DISCIPLINE AND CLASSROOM MANAGEMENT

Revised Edition

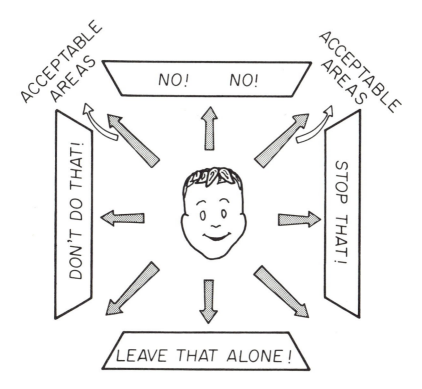

ACCEPTABLE AREAS

ACCEPTABLE AREAS

NO!   NO!

DON'T DO THAT!

STOP THAT!

LEAVE THAT ALONE!

D. Keith Osborn
Janie Dyson Osborn

EDUCATION ASSOCIATES
Athens, Georgia

ACKNOWLEDGEMENTS

We gratefully acknowledge the many persons who have made this publication possible. Among them are the professors who taught us, the college students we have worked with, our own children and our parents. But, most of all, the ones who really made this possible — the children who allowed us to learn from them in the many years we taught in the classroom.

We lovingly dedicate this book to our daughter, Michelle.

Send mail orders to:

Education Associates . . Box 8021 . . Athens, GA 30603

Cover Design: Jeanette M. Tuttle

ISBN #: Cloth Edition: 0-918772-09-5
        Paper Edition: 0-918772-10-9
Library of Congress Catalog Card Number: LC 81-66121

PREFACE

As beginning teachers both authors remember that the most difficult task was not mastery of subject matter content . . . rather it was learning how to deal effectively with children. There were situations when our best lesson plans were lost or wasted because of poor classroom management and control techniques. At times, an unruly kindergartener or a second grader can cause even the most competent teacher to question the wisdom of entering the teaching profession.

We should state at the outset that we definitely believe in discipline . . . we feel that if a teacher cares about a child she will provide guidance and discipline.

We should also state that we do *not* believe that discipline and classroom management are "magic" — therefore subject to some simple formula or mystical spell — nor is the discipline a "genetically endowed" trait. A "perfect" class with few discipline problems does not happen overnight. The student should be aware that discipline is a slow process and "hard to come by"; it demands constant supervision and a teacher who is "with-it". When you find a situation of this nature, take a closer look and you will find many techniques being implemented in the "hidden structure" of the class.

We believe that effective discipline and classroom management techniques are learned; therefore, a teacher can master the necessary skills. Chapter seven discusses twelve major factors which are necessary for effective discipline. Learning to approach discipline problems with these factors in mind will help resolve many problems which arise in the classroom milieu. However, this text is not a "cure all" . . . there will always be times when it will rain four days in a row and Mondays will always come after holidays!

Good luck,

Keith and Janie Osborn

iii

INTRODUCTION

We have used this text to supplement our beginning courses in education as well as a supplementary text in practicums where students are actually working with children. In our supervision with student teachers we have found the concepts discussed in the text are quite valuable in helping individuals gain useful classroom management techniques. After reading the text, the teacher can begin to diagnose her own approach to discipline and classroom management and see the consequences when she is inconsistent, lacks clarity, becomes stimulus bound, or engages in "over-kill" or "flip flops." Through studying the text, the teacher will begin to consider her approach to the "target child" in terms of "audience children."

There are a number of theoretical approaches to discipline. Frankly, some of them have little practical value for the classroom teacher. Every attempt has been made to present solid research results in meaningful, understandable terms which can be transferred to the classroom.

While the text utilizes four theoretical models (psychodynamic, behavior modification, social learning and field theory), discussions of these frames of reference are kept to a minimum. Our aim has been to help students in practical ways to work with children rather than to pontificate theoretical structures. However, it may be of interest to know that Chapter One and part of Chapter Two reflect the influence of the psychodynamic model. These chapters discuss the causality of behavior and ask the teacher to examine causative factors. Chapter Two particularly emphasizes the importance of the "emotional climate" in terms of the child's perception and acceptance of discipline.

Chapter Three discusses how children learn and reflects the behavior learning model. It shows how deviant behavior is learned and how new learning can occur with the subsequent modification of behavior. This chapter also discusses social learning theory and makes some generalizations concerning the modeling of behavior.

iv

Chapters Four and Seven draw from field theory and demonstrate the utilization of this theory in the actual classroom setting. This model draws from Lewin's postulate that behavior is equal to a function of the person in the environment. Kounin's research particularly shows the influence of Lewin's field theory.

Basically the psychodynamic view examines antecedent conditions with respect to deviate behavior while the other models are "ahistorical" being primarily concerned with the individual "in the present."

In this second edition, we have included two additional chapters. With mainstreaming, we felt it would be helpful to include a chapter particularly oriented to management tech niques and the exceptional child. The authors wish to gratefully acknowledge the help of Virginia A. Boyle, Ph.D. Before entering private practice as a clinical psychologist, Dr. Boyle was an Assistant Professor in Special Education at North Georgia College. In addition, she has served as Director of the Community Developmental Center for Children and Chief Psychologist at the Intense Learning Center in Brunswick, Georgia.

Like many others, we have become concerned with the onset of drugs in the elementary grades. Our work with teachers has made us realize that often they know little of drugs or the drug culture. However, drugs have become so pervasive that they are affecting the school and the classroom. Chapter Five was included to provide the teacher with more knowledge about the various types of drugs, the incidence of drug abuse and some concrete suggestions which the teacher and parent can do. Since drugs are just beginning to filter down into the elementary grades, we have emphasized the importance of prevention.

One final word. In order to ease reading of the text, we have referred to the teacher as "she" and to the child as "he."

Table of Contents

*Chapter Six is written by Virginia A. Boyle, Ph.D.

Chapter One

Will The Real Problem Child Please Stand Up?

During the discussion period following any lecture on discipline many questions are raised. Usually, at least one teacher will direct a question to the speaker similar to the following: "I have a boy in my class who is quite aggressive. He is eight years old. . . . " It is, of course, impossible for the lecturer to answer meaningfully this type of question without further knowledge of the particular situation. Certainly many factors are involved. For example: What does the teacher mean by aggression? Is the aggression expressed internally? What is the frequency of the aggression displayed? What behavioral acts lead to the aggression? We could ask many other questions in connection with the teacher's problem and still remain unable to provide an adequate answer.

In many instances, the teacher who originally made the inquiry holds the answer to her own question — and the solution to her own problem. However, she must be willing to conduct a search within herself and to utilize the resources at her command. Many answers to behavior

1

problems lay fallow within the teacher's own experiences; in her sensitivity to particular situations and in her ability as an observer.

In helping the teacher seek answers for dealing with a particular child, we would like to propose a series of questions. In utilizing this approach, the teacher will usually determine the source of the problem. In many instances, the solution may be embodied within her answers to the questions.

Am I The Problem?

Generally speaking, the more you know about a person, the better you can understand him. While this statement is not a "scientific law," it is certainly a good rule. This maxim applies to the children you teach — and, of course, this rule applies to you, too!

How much do you know about yourself? You probably visit your dentist and physician regularly for a physical examination; but when was the last time you gave yourself a "Teacher Check-up"?

In order to understand the child's feelings, the teacher must recognize her own. To be able to empathize with a child's feelings of anger, the teacher should be aware of her own feelings of hostility and the events which cause her to become angry. In order to understand and accept a child's feelings of anxiety; the teacher must be willing to recognize these same feelings within herself. The teacher should be cognizant of the fact that unresolved conflicts in her own life can filter into the teaching situation and have an effect on her pupils.

The purpose of this section is to help the reader engage in some *self-analysis* to determine *one* possible source of a potential problem. Often we find that some apparent "problem children" are, in reality, adults with a problem. Usually, if we can resolve the adult problem — the child problem will resolve itself. After reading and studying this section, you may wish to refer to the assessment items in Appendix D.

2

1. *Why am I teaching anyway?*

This question is so basic that it should be answered by every person *prior* to entering the profession of teaching. What personal needs does teaching fulfill? Sometimes an individual becomes a teacher in order to dominate and control others. Some persons want to work with children because they are unable to relate to adults. Needless to say, these are not valid reasons for entering the teaching profession.

Some teachers tend to identify too greatly with their pupils. In doing so the teacher's ego becomes so highly involved that every pupil's success is a personal triumph. Every pupil failure becomes a personal failure and rebuff to the teacher. The net result is a "pressure cooker" classroom setting in which children suffer under high teacher demands and unreasonable expectations. In examining her philosophy the teacher should ask, "What is really significant; what really counts in my teaching?"

2. *Is "what really counts" significant?*

At times situations can arise and teachers become bogged down in minutiae. We once knew a teacher who wanted all the children to place their pencils on the desks with the erasers pointed in the same direction. We have known a few kindergarten teachers who were unhappy when the slightest paint was spilled. Some of these teachers felt they had "problem children." Instead, the children had compulsive, neurotic teachers.

Once, when conducting some research on discipline, we developed the category, "too much issue" to describe this type of adult. In our study we encountered parents and teachers who often made a big issue out of a small problem. In our observations we saw a father spank a three year old who let the screen door slam; we observed a high school teacher give five hours of extra work because a boy left his seat to sharpen a pencil. While these matters can be disturbing, we felt that the adults were creating "too much issue."

3

3. What do children do that upsets me?

In many ways, this question is the most significant one in our checklist. Remember to consider things which cause minor upsets. Little problems, like small bills, can really add up. For example, some teachers become overly concerned with time. They become rigid in their adherence to a schedule. If a child falls behind . . . the teacher becomes irritated and forgets her real purpose in teaching. Everyone has minor prejudices and these do effect the way we deal with people. Some teachers are overly concerned with manner of dress and may unconsciously punish children who do not dress well. Some adults are prejudiced against fatness, cuteness, ugliness and poor language patterns. In a number of cases, the child does not have the problem — rather, the teacher has a prejudice which she must learn to handle. Often, merely recognizing the problem makes it become more manageable.

4. Is my approach to children clouded by my own childhood experience?

It is impossible to keep your own childhood experiences from entering into your approach to children. Often these experiences can be helpful in our vicarious understanding of others. At times, however, they can interfere. As mentioned in the statement above, our own prejudices can effect the way we work with children.

Often parents want their children to succeed in areas where they failed as children. They push and pressure children to be popular, date sooner, read better or make the first string in Little League football. The mature adult is capable of accepting other selves for what they are, rather than what the adult self would like them to be. A nervous, distraught child is often a normal child who has become upset and anxious as a result of misguided adult pressures. Guiding learning means working with children so they can discover, create and develop to their fullest capacity.

4

5. *Am I tired or upset?*

One rainy Monday in my first year of teaching the morning was going particularly bad. The children seemed unusually noisy and argumentative and I was beginning to question the wisdom of my decision to enter the teaching profession. At that moment Mavis grabbed Cindy's book and I grabbed Mavis and said sternly, "No, No, No!!" Mavis shrugged her shoulders and said plaintively, "Teacher, do you realize you have been saying, 'No' all morning?"

When you think you have a problem, ask yourself, "Is this just one of those days?" You know — we all have "those days." Unless care is taken, the tired or worried teacher creates her own problem situations. Lack of sleep, concern over the illness of a loved one, unpaid bills, four days of rain — many factors can contribute to making the work situation difficult. During these periods — whenever the teacher is fatigued or worried — even minor problems can assume major proportions.

In summary.

Be honest with yourself and in your approach to the questions raised in this chapter. Answering the items discussed may provide insight into that so-called "problem child." You may wish to refer to the assessment items in Appendix D. They are designed to help you see if you are meeting your goals in terms of discipline. Despite low pay and minor problems, teaching is a challenging rewarding profession. One of the most satisfying experiences is to watch a child grow socially and intellectually. If relating to children in this way does not excite you and "turn you on" — seriously review your answers to the first question.

Determining The Problem:
A Case Study

When the teacher satisfies herself that she is *not* the problem, she should begin to gather information which will prove useful in diagnosing the child's trouble. There are three major considerations in studying individual behavior. One is an empirical question: "How does a person actually behave in a given situation?" The second issue is a theoretical one, "Why does he behave as he does?" The third is a practical question: "What can I do to help this child?"

While it is not the purpose of this treatise to discuss data collection in detail, this section will provide some guidelines which can help the teacher answer the initial question — "How does the child actually behave?" Prior to implementing any detailed plan of action the teacher should conduct a simple child study. Three essential ingredients are needed in preparing such a study: description, observation and interpretation.

1. A description of the child.

The first part of a child study should concern itself with a general description of the child. The birthdate, sex, height, weight, overall physical condition and appearance should be included. If the child is taking medication, has any allergies or unusual physical maladies — these should be noted. There should be a short statement concerning the child's parents and siblings. If there are any unusual home circumstances (parents divorced; father not permitted to visit youngster; child lives with grandparent) these should be included in your general statement. In addition the teacher should provide a short summary describing the child physically, socially, emotionally and intellectually. Any unusual interests, abilities or attitudes in these areas should be mentioned. The purpose of the general description is to provide the reader with a "feel" for the youngster being observed.

2. Observation.

The teacher should make a number of observations of the child. A good observation should present an accurate account of the child's behavior. A person reading the observation should be able to visualize the same picture as the person who observed the original event. The following suggestions will be helpful in gathering a complete and accurate record.

★ Date each observation and indicate the time of day.
★ Indicate the duration of an event or events.
    — How long did the child cry; have his thumb in his mouth?
    —How long was the child involved in block building; in reading a book; listening to phonograph records?
★ Indicate persons and events which are reinforcing.
    — Best friend; favorite friends.
    — Preferred activities; favorite game.
★ Include actual dialogue, where possible.
    — *Instead of:* T. told child to leave room and she refused.
    — *Report:* T. said: "Leave this room immediately and do not come back until you learn to behave." Gloria threw her book on the floor, stamped her foot and said, "I didn't do it and you can't make me leave!"
★ Describe the situation in which the behavior took place.
    — In some instances it may be helpful to make a drawing of the room, the location of the children, the location of the equipment, the location of the teacher.
★ Include full details of the activity.
    — *Instead of:* He played in the doll corner.
    — *Report:* Mike sat in the doll corner with three small rubber dolls. He placed the mother doll in the living room area and put the baby doll in the high chair. He took the father doll and said to me, "This is the papa; he is going to spank the baby for going wee-wee."
★ Describe actions, rather than labeling.
    — Avoid the use of labels. For example: Fun-loving, spoiled brat, possessive, lazy, introverted. Rather report the actual behavior which has occurred.
    — *Instead of:* Brenda is highly dependent.
    — *Report:* Brenda will not leave my side during free

7

play. If my hands are not engaged in actually holding something, Brenda will take my hand and not let go of it.

★ Avoid pseudo-descriptive terms.
— Some terms do not describe. However, they appear to be bona-fide descriptions, and give the reader a psychological "set" (prejudgment) concerning a child. Examples: He is always late . . . she never does her work . . . she is highly possessive . . . he is just naturally lazy . . . he is very stubborn and always refuses to cooperate.

One method of observing would be to gather several short five to ten minute samples of each day over a period of one to two weeks. The time samples should be taken during different segments of the day in order to achieve a balanced picture of the child's behavior.

A technique suggested by Fleming (1973), the shadow study, is a useful method in observing the child's behavior over an entire day. The student is "shadowed" all day long and recordings are made at fifteen minute intervals. The observer keeps two types of records: the student's responses and the setting in which the activity took place.

3. Interpretive comments.

A case study should also contain the teacher's interpretive comments. However, these evaluative statements should be placed at the end of the report and labelled so the reader understands the statements are interpretive, rather than actual descriptions of behavior. The appendix contains two observations which illustrate one method of gathering data. For the student who wishes to study methods of observation and data collection in greater detail, consult the references in the bibliography. The books by Cohen and Stern, Gordon, Fleming and Rowen will be particularly helpful.

Physical and Psychosocial Considerations

The preceding section addressed itself to the question: "How does the child actually behave in a given situation?" In many instances day-to-day observations of general behavior will provide the teacher with sufficient information to plan appropriate ways of working with the child. For example, daily observations may reveal that the teacher is using inappropriate reinforcement techniques —or that her techniques are inconsistent — or lack clarity. The case study of Sam (Chapter Three) shows the value of observation in planning strategies for altering behavior. Observation # 1 in Appendix C illustrates how observation can provide insight into problems which arise in the course of an ordinary school day.

However, if the difficulty still persists, we suggest the teacher carefully study the following questions which deal with rather specific physical and psychosocial considerations. The remainder of the chapter will provide some insight into why the child behaves as he does. The chapter will also present suggestions on what can be done when solutions are beyond the scope of the educator's training.

Except for the first item (the child's physical condition) the questions are not presented in any order of importance. The teacher should examine all the questions which are raised in this section and investigate all areas as an integral part of her overall evaluation.

1. Is the child physically sound?

Many so-called behavior problems hide behind poor health. We have known several good teachers who were looking for psychological symptoms and discovered poor vision, poor hearing or poor metabolism instead.

Once we were visiting a Head Start center in Boston and the teachers asked us to observe Frank, a four year old who was a "biter." As we watched it was obvious that Frank was indeed quite "nervous." He seemed constantly in motion and bit two children that morning. Coincidental to our visit that day a dentist was at the center conducting

9

preliminary dental examinations.

At noon the head teacher and dentist had lunch together. During this period the dentist said to the teacher: "I would like to schedule an appointment for Frank as soon as possible. The condition of his mouth and gums is terrible. He is in constant pain." Then the dentist added casually, "Of course, I know you are surely aware of his poor physical condition — because the pain is obviously causing him to be highly active and nervous."

Two months later we saw Frank's teacher. She informed us that following substantial dental work Frank had "calmed down" and stopped biting.

A child who is mentally retarded can present problems which appear to have psychological origins. Since about thirty children in every 1,000 are diagnosed as mentally retarded, the teacher should be alerted to this possibility. A mentally deficient child will never catch up to the average child his age. As he grows older, he falls farther behind. However, Dittman points out (1975, p. 139): "Except in cases of extreme mental retardation, parents and teachers can help mentally retarded children develop . . . how his family and others treat a mentally retarded child has much to do with whether or not the child can remain emotionally healthy and well adjusted."

Often mental retardation is diagnosed during infancy —but many children are not identified until nursery, kindergarten or public school. There have been instances where an alert teacher detected the problem after it had been overlooked by parents and medical personnel. (See Chapter 6 for a discussion on the exceptional child.)

Some children experience illnesses which necessitate frequent absences from school. It is not unusual for the child to become an "onlooker" since establishing and maintaining friendships is difficult with intermittent attendance. In some instances the child may become aggressive in order to gain attention from other children. With such cases the teacher may need to make special adjustments to ease the child's re-entry into the classroom and to help him feel he is a part of the group.

Various physiological deficiencies can also effect be-

10

havior. One of the biggest "problem creators" is lack of sleep. Too often parents allow children to stay up late and watch television. A recent survey by the National Association for Better Broadcasting found that seven million children (ages 2-11) watched television as late as 11 PM. When a child is tired and lacks sleep he becomes irritable and cranky.

Some children are taking medication or a combination of drugs as perscribed by the pediatrician or psychiatrist. At the beginning of the year determine which children are on medication and the type of medication used. Individuals who are taking "common" drugs may display unusual and even bizarre symptoms. Ask the parent if there are any unusual symptoms (like drowsiness, slurry speech, irritability, poor coordination, dilated pupils) associated with ingestion of the drug.

If this is your first year of teaching in a particular school system, determine the policy concerning dispensing drugs during school hours. Schools *do* vary in their procedures on drug intake. Some systems allow the teacher to dispense drugs; other prefer that this task be delegated to the school nurse or principal. Most systems will not dispense drugs without written permission from the parent or physician.

Unfortunately you may have a youngster who is taking an unauthorized or illegal drug. Drug abuse has become a problem of epidemic proportion in the United States and some children as early as eight to ten years of age are involved. A sad truth is that an initial drug encounter may occur on school grounds. Unusual changes in behavior —a drugged, sluggish appearance, unusual euphoria, slurred speech, a quiet demeanor — may all be symptoms of drug use. Because of the rapid escalation in the drug problem, an entire chapter (Chapter Five) is devoted to this situation and specific suggestions are provided to the teacher.

Inadequate nutrition can also effect behavior. A teacher from Alabama related the following incident:

"One summer I taught in the Head Start program. Each morning we served breakfast to the children because we knew that they were not receiving an adequate meal before coming to the center.

"That fall, when I returned to my public school position, most of the Head Start children were placed in my first grade class. However, I was shocked at the drastic difference in the behavior of these children.

"In the public school setting they seemed less active, sluggish and docile. I began to wonder if, somehow, the more formal school setting was inhibiting their behavior. As time passed, however, I began to notice a slight change. The children did begin to become more active and attentive — but, to my amazement, this behavior change occurred only in the afternoon!

"Several weeks later it struck me! The increase in activity was occurring immediately following the lunch hour! After consulting with the lunchroom manager, we made arrangements to provide the children with a breakfast snack when they arrived each morning. Within a short period of time a noticeable change in the children's behavior had taken place."

Read (1976) reports that almost twenty percent of American children under six years of age consume less than the recommended daily intake of calories. In low income families almost one-third of the young children have insufficient caloric intake. Pre-teens and adolescents also have poor eating habits. Some teenagers attempt to survive on a diet of potato chips and cola drinks. While the effects of moderate malnutrition are not completely understood, studies suggest that malnourished children tend to lag in behavioral development, motor skill performance, reading ability, concentration and motivation.

It is almost impossible for the child to learn when his hunger needs are not satisfied. A hungry child is nervous, listless, poorly motivated and disruptive. Several states have begun to recognize this problem and have legislation requiring schools to provide both breakfast and lunch to students.

Some physical illnesses, like hypoglycemia, may carry symptoms which appear psychological and manifest themselves in peculiar behavior. A child with dyslexia may be placed under considerable pressure because the adult feels the child is not motivated to learn. Unless the teacher is fully aware of the physical problem she may mistakenly respond to the psychological symptoms and delay the necessary medical treatment. Recent nutritional research raises questions which suggest that some food colorings and food additives can also effect growth and behavior.

We would strongly suggest to teachers that if they suspect a severe behavior problem they initially consult the school nurse or physician to determine whether or not the problem has its etiology in a physical area.

2. What is the child's cultural background?

The term "culture" is used here in a broad sense and includes children representing various backgrounds and social situations. Problems can arise when children come from a home possessing values which are at variance with the teacher or the school system. In a study with day care families Elardo and Caldwell (1973) found that one of the important differences between teachers and parents was in the area of aggression. While the teachers discouraged fighting, parents felt their children should be aggressive and defend their rights. Caldwell (1977, p. 10) reports: "We have had parents pick their son up from school and then drive around the school campus looking for another child who supposedly had insulted their son — in order that, when the other boy was located the son could get out of the car and beat the boy up. Similarly, we had a child whose parents had 'dared' him to come home from school without having beaten up the little boy who threw sand in his sister's eyes while they were playing together the previous weekend."

In another situation a teacher acquaintance had asked her third grade students to write an essay entitled, "My friend, the Policeman." One child responded, "But Ms. Bennett, the policeman ain't no friend of mine. He put my mother in jail."

A teacher from Michigan shared the following: Lauren

13

was a kindergarten child who seemed unable to share. When playing in the doll corner, she would gather all the dolls to herself and not allow anyone else to touch them. If Lauren was at a table coloring, she would hoard all the crayons. The teacher made an interesting discovery during a home visit. The home was completely devoid of toys, play materials or other items which a young child would enjoy. Lauren had almost no previous experience with play materials and, consequently, wanted them "all to herself."

Once at The Merrill-Palmer Institute, a visiting teacher asked the Counseling Service for help with a problem child. The "psychological" problem was, in fact, a cultural one. The child (who was presenting real behavior problems to his teacher) had come from the "old country" one year earlier. His behavior was quite (culturally) acceptable to his parents. After some counseling with both parents and the teacher, an acceptable resolution was reached and the problem ceased to exist.

Teachers should be aware of the religious backgrounds of their students since some religions place restrictions on the activities of their members. These restrictions may make children reticent to participate in some school activities. For example, some religions prohibit pledging allegiance to the flag, the celebration of any holidays, including birthdays or the viewing of motion pictures — even if educational in nature. Some religious organizations may accept movement education but prohibit dancing.

3. What is the child's learning ability?

A behavior problem may really be a learning problem. Research suggests that when a pupil's level of aspiration is incompatible (by being either too high or too low) with his performance ability, there is pressure to "leave the field" of learning. In our interviews with children we encountered youngsters who were "bored" with school. In a number of instances the child was capable of a high level of performance but teacher expectations were slight. As a result the child quickly finished his assignments and drifted into trouble.

Obviously the reverse holds true. Some children have a level of aspiration which far exceeds their performance ability. One fall we interviewed Ralph, an eleventh grader, who indicated his desire to become a medical doctor. His school grades were quite poor — mostly C's and D's. We asked him how he thought he could enter college with such poor grades. He replied that he was sure his grades would improve his junior year. In the Spring we were conducting some follow-up interviews on the same children. We learned that Ralph had dropped out of school and was working in a car wash. Unfortunately no one at the school had been able to help Ralph determine a more realistic level of apsiration. As a result he simply "left the field" of learning.

Some children have physiological problems which make learning difficult. This child may appear to be disruptive in a deep psychological sense. Kephart (1971, p. 5) presents an enlightening description of this youngster:

"To most teachers, as well as parents, the slow learning child is a complete enigma. One day he learns the classroom material to perfection; the next he seems to have forgotten every bit of it. In one activity he excels all other children; in the next he performs like a two-year-old. His behavior is unpredictable and almost violent in its intensity. He is happy to the point of euphoria but, the next moment, he is sad to the point of depression."

In the section, "Is the child physically sound," we mentioned dyslexia. Usually children with dyslexia are not mentally retarded. However, children diagnosed as dyslexic often encounter pressure under the erroneous idea that they are not motivated to learn. Some may become highly upset since they cannot read as well as their classmates. While physicians do not have a specific cure for dyslexia, qualified reading specialists can often help the child.

A word of warning: Often "slow learner" and "dyslexia" are used as "catch all" terms for any general problem or reading disability. The teacher should avoid the pitfall of labelling a problem since a label can provide "false comfort" and delay parents in conducting a search for some workable alternatives. In such situations the teacher should recognize her own limitations and be prepared to make a referral to professionals trained to work with specific problems beyond the scope of the average teacher. The reader is referred to Chapter Six. This chapter is specifically addressed to management techniques and the exceptional child.

In the meantime the teacher should learn to focus on the specific problem which is upsetting to the child. If she can isolate the specific trouble and systematically work to effect a solution — she may solve the problem or make definite headway toward its ultimate resolution.

4. Is this a case of school "culture shock?"

Four out of five children move to a new residence every 18 months. In many cases the child also moves to a new school. Teachers should recognize that a new home and a new school can represent "culture shock" for the child. Usually the move means learning new surroundings, making new friends and adjusting to a new teacher.

The following example is fairly typical: Ginger, aged seven, had recently transferred to a new school. Her parents reported that she resisted going to school each morning and was having difficulty sleeping. Ginger merely said, "I don't like school any more!" After a lengthy investigation and consultation with the new teacher the real problem emerged. In the new school the teacher expected the children to use cursive handwriting. In Ginger's old school the children used manuscript; cursive handwriting was not taught until the third grade. Ginger did not understand cursive writing but was afraid to tell the teacher for fear of reprisal.

"Culture shock" can occur within the same system when a child moves from one grade to the next, as seen in the following example:

Darlene had a third grade teacher who gave high grades and required little from her pupils. Darlene received all A's from this teacher. The following year she moved to a new school in another section of the city. Darlene's fourth grade teacher demanded a great deal from her pupils and had high grading standards. In reviewing third grade material the first few weeks, several things were apparent: Darlene was spending long hours preparing her homework; her test scores were C's and D's. Darlene became nervous and cried when it was time to go to school. Because of the difference in performance from the previous year, the teacher requested a conference with the parents. This conference revealed curriculum differences between the two schools. Recognizing the problem the teacher became more empathic and provided individualized work until Darlene was able to "catch up" with her classmates.

5. Is the child reacting to some unknown situation in the home environment?

Parents can pressure their children and the result can manifest itself in the classroom. For example:

Beth was an extremely bright five year old. An only child, her mother was an attorney; her father a psychologist. The parent's academic expectations for Beth were quite high. At two years of age she loved classical music, her parents taught her to read when she was four. In kindergarten her language facility was that of an adult. Late in the kindergarten year she was reading at the sixth grade level.

However, Beth did not like kindergarten. She was unable to get along with her classmates. She tried to boss them but they would not conform to her demands. She was unable to share with others and spent most of the class day in the corner reading a book. At group time she was inattentive or wanted to dominate a conversation. When not given her way, she would throw a temper tantrum —stamping her feet, screaming and crying. For the most part, Beth only worked well with the teacher and was unable to communicate with the children.

In a conference the teacher shared her problem with the

17

parents. The parents agreed that Beth's behavior was such that she needed psychological help. Several months later (in the first grade) Beth began to improve. She learned to share and was beginning to relate more meaningfully with other children.

One afternoon the father stopped by to see the kindergarten teacher. He happily related Beth's progress and then added: "We just expected too much of Beth academically. We spent too much time teaching her to read but never gave her the opportunity to socialize with others."

Divorce can create problems which affect the child's performance in school. Statistics reveal that one marriage in three ends in divorce — thus there are very few classrooms which are immune to this situation.

Studies on divorce indicate that children do suffer as a result. They may make high demands upon the teacher when a divorce is in progress. Our own observation is that psychologically the child may reach out to the teacher and demand more attention. An interpretation of this behavior might be that the child is seeking strength and reassurance in the one adult in his life who seemingly has remained stable and predictable . . . in this case that adult may be the teacher.

There is no such thing as a victimless divorce. One study on preschool children found that nearly 50% of the children involved in a divorce displayed significant psychological problems one year following the divorce. Some school-aged children respond to divorce with extreme melancholy and sadness, fear, feelings of loss and deprivation. Studies suggest that during this traumatic period boys become highly aggressive and disturbed. Children may fear they are being rejected and displaced.

A divorce can create many changes and new problems. Father is absent from the home; father takes the child for a visit . . . or, if father is awarded custody, then mother will see the child on a limited basis. If one of the parents moves from the city, then the child will face even more limited visitation from the parent who was not awarded custody. In some cases a new stepparent or a housemate may enter the home; in other situations the child may move in with the grandparents and only see the parents on a limited or haphazard basis. Custody fights and financial hassles over alimony are extremely traumatic and can severely threaten children and affect their behavior. Skeen and McKenry have an excellent article on the role of the teacher in facilitating a child's adjustment to divorce. In their article they summarize many of the behavioral reactions which one may witness in children. They also provide an excellent bibliography for the teacher and parent as well as appropriate books for preschool and school aged children.

The teacher must be aware that children do not come to school in a vacuum. Mother's illness, Daddy's new job and a new baby sister all attend school in the mind of the child. The problems of the home do come to school.

6. Is the child reacting to some unknown situation in the school environment?

Problems can arise in school, but away from the pupil's classroom. In these instances the teacher may be totally unaware of the total Gestalt and its effect on the child. A strict, irritable bus driver and a bus load of rowdy, boisterous children is enough to make a quiet shy first grader wish he did not have to go to school. Initially the three incidents which follow were quite mysterious:

Quite suddenly and for no apparent reason, Cheryl, aged four, did not like to attend nursery school on Thursdays. After some questioning, the teacher discovered that the Thursday car pool mother allowed the family cat to ride in the car. While the other children enjoyed this guest passenger, its presence was terrifying to Cheryl.

Winston, a third grader, had recently moved to a new school. After two weeks, Winston told his parents he wanted to move back to their old neighborhood. When he was asked why he was unhappy, Winston would become uncommunicative. The teacher could report nothing in the classroom which was contributing to this unhappiness. However, she had observed that every afternoon, during the final period, Winston would become nervous, upset and highly active. A short time later (and quite by accident) the teacher discovered that every afternoon on the way home, Winston was being beaten by a group of fourth grade boys.

Virginia, a fifth grader, would not go to the bathroom. Investigation showed that some kids were smoking pot in the girl's restroom and this behavior upset Virginia. However, peer pressure made her afraid to tell the teacher.

7. What is the child's role with his peer group?

The peer group can be a powerful influence. In our camp one summer we had a nine year old, Teddy, whose behavior seemed incomprehensible. At breakfast Teddy would often take his cereal bowl, turn it over his head and allow its contents to dribble down his face. Whenever possible, the counselor would prevent this activity; however, if the transgression occurred, Teddy was immediately punished. It was also obvious that the boys did not think it funny, since the visual impression of the incident usually caused several of his cabin mates to become ill and rush from the breakfast table.

One day the counselor overheard some of the campers discussing a "breakfast date with Teddy." Investigation revealed that on each occasion when Teddy performed the cereal stunt, the boys took Teddy behind the cabin and beat him. Armed with this knowledge the counselor approached Teddy and informed him that he knew about the "breakfast date" and said:

Counselor: "Teddy, if you would just stop spilling that cereal on your head, those guys would quit beating you."

Teddy: *(smiling)* "Yeah, that's right."

Counselor: "Well, doesn't it hurt you when they beat you?"

Teddy: *(still smiling)* "Yeah."

Counselor: "Well?"

Teddy: "Hey, man . . . can't you see who is the center of attention — it's me!"

Obviously this youngster had a serious problem. It took

the counselor a long time before he was able to convince Teddy that he could become a vital part of the group without resorting to negative, destructive behavior.

In the classroom setting we see a similar problem in the child who appoints himself the "class clown." Since he has not learned other acceptable methods for effecting entry into the peer group, this child "performs" in silly, bizarre ways.

There are many other behaviors which may indicate the child is limited in knowledge of social approaches which can aid in gaining acceptance by the peer group. The child who becomes the "class gossip," the highly aggressive child, the "class bully" . . . these are not problem children in the classical sense; rather they are youngsters who need guidance in developing and perfecting social skills.

In recent years, the peer group has become a powerful influence in the use of drugs and alcohol. Many children report being ostracized by the group if they do not participate in drinking alcohol or smoking grass. This type of peer pressure is discussed in Chapter Five.

8. Is the pupil going through a developmental phase?

Sometimes behavior problems are developmental in nature. Refusing to sit at one table (if you are an eight year old boy — and the table is filled with girls) is probably a developmental problem, rather than a disciplinary one.

A three year old experiencing difficulties in sharing may say, "I know we share — but I want it!!" This child may appear to be selfish in the eyes of the adult. But more likely he is involved in the throes of egocentrism and is cognitively unable to perceive that someone else should want the same item he desires. His inability to perceptually imagine the feelings of others makes sharing difficult . . . he sees only that he wants the item in question.

Pre-adolescent boys and girls often engage in minor aggressive activity. The boys pick at the girls and push them; the girls hit the boys. In spite of loud voices, vigorous protests and feinted injuries, this activity is usually harmless. Actually one is witnessing early attempts at boy-girl relations — and these initial overtures represent uncultivated preludes of later, more serious relationships. In the middle school and high school one may encounter "teacher baiting." The child purposely resorts to behaviors which will assure a negative response on the part of the teacher. In this situation if the teacher "takes the bait" and verbally attacks the instigator, she creates a minor "folk hero" for the class. Actually an inverse correlation may result — thus the more upset the teacher becomes, the greater the degree of admiration for the child involved.

Before The Doctor Arrives

In conducting a case study and in gathering data on the specific questions raised in the preceding section, it may become apparent that the child has a problem or a series of problems which are clearly beyond the scope of the teacher's training. In such situations the teacher should recognize her own limitations and seek outside help. If the teacher must make a referral to the visiting teacher or the school psychologist, her description and observations will be extremely helpful.

In addition to the teacher's child study, the following specific information will be useful to any professional who will ultimately work with the child.

1. Relationships.
   ★ To whom does the child relate?
   — Person orientation: Does he relate better to a particular friend, one parent, a special teacher, only to adults?

   — Object orientation: Does he relate primarily to nonhumans (his pet, animals) . . . Displays preference for reading books over being with people; would rather play with blocks than other children.

   ★ How does he relate?
   — Leader, follower, dependent, dominant, submissive?

2. How is free time used?
   ★ Creatively, destructively, for tension reduction, likes clean activities only; messy activities only. In what areas is free time spent?

3. Control system.
   ★ Does child know right from wrong?
   ★ Does he feel guilty — very tense?
   ★ Over controlled?
   ★ Lacks spontaniety?

4. What is his orientation to reality?
   ★ Appropriate, inappropriate?
   ★ Daydreams, avoids reality.
   ★ Tells stories, prevaricates.
   ★ Seems dazed, out of touch.

5. How does he communicate?
   ★ Friendly, outgoing?
   ★ Hostile, angry (chip on shoulder)?
   ★ Very quiet, non-communicative?
   ★ Absence of any emotion?

6. How does he feel about himself?
   ★ Highly egocentric?
   ★ Defensive, denies problems?
   ★ Regressive (acts younger than he is)?
   ★ Does not like self (says he is bad, no good)?

Supervisory Conference

When the teacher has determined that the child's problem is clearly beyond her expertise as an educator, she should arrange a conference with her principal or immediate supervisor. Questions which need to be resolved include: Who will conference with parents? What referral suggestions will be made? Who will actually make the referral? Who will follow-up on the referral? What will the teacher's role be during this period?

It is recognized that in some small communities a day care director or private school operator may not have large social agencies available for referral. In these situations we would make the following suggestions of persons or agencies who can advise the private operator on possibilities for referral.

Today, through federal grants, many counties have a mental health clinic or an office of family services. The personnel in these clinics are trained and are happy to help educators with problems. In very small communities, where a mental health center does not exist, there are usually three additional possibilities.

The county health department usually has a person with some training in psychology. Often there is a nurse or psychiatric social worker who can provide information. A second source is your own physician. Most physicians have had some psychiatric training and are knowledgeable concerning available sources of referral in the area. The third source is your church pastor. Many clergymen (particularly young ministers) have received some training in pastoral counseling and can give advice and referral information.

Learning Objectives For Chapter One:

After reading Chapter One, "Will the real problem child please stand up," the reader should be able to:

1. Analyze the extent to which she is creating a discipline problem within the classroom.
2. List child behaviors which are upsetting to her personally.

3. Determine problems from her own early childhood experiences which may interfere with her approach to teaching children.
4. Write anecdotal observations in descriptive terms, separating actual behaviors from interpretative comments.
5. List criteria necessary to insure objective observation.
6. Identify physical and psychosocial considerations in normal children which may lead to discipline problems. (The text lists eight major considerations; the reader should be able to discuss each consideration and its implications as a potential problem.)
7. Determine when a discipline problem is beyond the scope of the educator.
8. Write clinical observations in descriptive terms which can be used by a psychiatrist, psychologist, social worker or visiting teacher.
9. Determine when and how to make a referral.

Chapter Two

A Double Continuum — A New Look At Discipline

Historically, one might view the attitudes of parents and teachers toward discipline as simply a matter of control. For most of history, disciplinary action toward children has been quite strict. In an effort to regulate their efforts, children have been severely beaten, dunked in cold water, deprived of food, burned, abandoned and even killed. Historians have noted that until the 19th century, most of the world's child population was actually abused.

The Control Continuum

With the beginning of the child development movement in the early part of the 20th century some authorities suggested that strong unreasonable discipline might create psychological problems in children. Others, during this Victorian era, believed that "children should be seen and not heard," and adhered to the maxim of "spare the rod and spoil the child." In the years which followed experts have aligned themselves along a "control continuum." Figure 2.1 shows this range of thought.

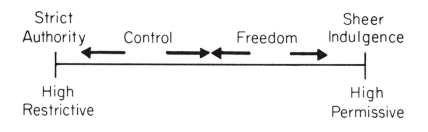

Figure 2.1

Over the years the discipline pendulum has swung back and forth — alternating between the advocates for a strict authoritarian approach and persons suggesting little or no regulation. In the 20s and 30s, the Watsonian point of view (with scheduled feeding) was in vogue; in the 40s, 50s, and 60s, the Freudians — along with Dr. Spock (and demand feeding), had their day. Popular magazines reflected this swing of the pendulum with articles like: "Free expression breeds free children" or "Let's go back to the woodshed!" and "Put the lid on the ID!"

As young professionals we well remember trying to cope with both points of view. Both positions had strong arguments in their favor, but each viewpoint also contained disadvantages. In an article entitled, "Permissiveness Re-examined" (Osborn, 1968, pp. 108-109), the problems with each extreme were examined. The following section is adapted from that article.

Strict authoritarian

Very early in life the child begins to explore his environment by crawling, walking, hitting and knocking over things. During these periods of experimentation it is

27

only human nature that the parent begins to exert pressures in the form of control. By "control pressures" we are referring to such verbal expressions as: "No, not now," "Leave that alone," "I will do that"; or to physical pressures like a tap on the hand or an old fashion spanking. Unfortunately, simple control of behavior via the techniques of threatening and physical punishment is so simple and expedient, the adult can fall into the trap of hollering and hitting for any minor offense. Unless the adult is careful, the child may be surrounded (overpowered may be the better term) by a "Wall of No." Figure 2.2 illustrates the "Wall of No."

In the illustration shown in Figure 2.2 we can see that the child is so tightly controlled that he cannot express his thoughts and feelings outwardly — he must turn these feelings inward to himself. (Psychologists would refer to this mechanism of defense as "repression.") Confronted with this "Wall of No," the child begins to learn: "I do not have to think, the adults will do my thinking for me." "I

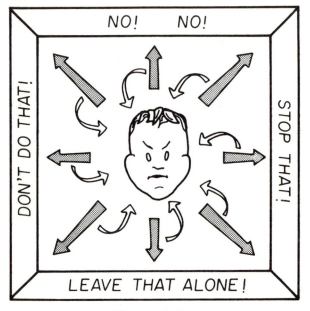

Figure 2.2

cannot say what I feel; I must be bad because I am always wrong in whatever I do." "If I do this, I will get a spanking!" In other words, we get a picture of a child who cannot respond freely — a child who is unable to allow himself to have feelings. *Granted, we have a child who is learning; but we have a child who is learning to respond out of fear of punishment rather than out of understanding of the situation.*

In order to clarify the strict authoritarian system let us use an example. Suppose you have a young child who runs into the street. Under the strict authoritarian mode you would "whale the daylights" out of the child if he ventures near a road or thoroughfare. If the parent performs this spanking without fail, she will have accomplished her objective — at least in part. That is, the child will not go into the street. However, we need to ask, "Why will the child stay out of the street?" Because of the fear of a spanking, not because of the inherent dangers of playing in the street. This learning works whenever the authority figure is present; but when the authority leaves (and the fear of punishment is removed) the child may dart into the street.

We can see that under such conditions healthy personality development is held back — free expression and autonomy are not allowed to develop. If the young child is to explore and discover, he must be allowed to discover his own limitations and learn adequate self-control.

Sheer indulgence

Years ago, the problem of the strict authoritarian approach seemed quite clear. Unfortunately clinical psychologists and teachers often left parents dangling at this point in a discussion on discipline. With the words "free expression" ringing in their ears, parents often became completely immobilized by any action which would demand an authoritarian stance.

We see this dilemma reflected in the following example: At a recent PTA meeting one of the parents remarked, "Psychologists have told us so much about personality development and permissiveness that I am afraid to do

29

anything to my child lest I injure his personality." At the same meeting another mother said, "My two year old hits the TV screen with a wooden mallet. I want to stop him but I do not want to hinder this freedom business while he is in this stage of autonomy."

Unfortunately, the course of immobility on the part of the parent or the teacher can be just as damaging to the child as the adult who totally engages in a strict authoritarian approach. We might use the term "sheer indulgence" to describe this mode of activity. Figure 2.3 shows this behavior.

In Figure 2.3 we see that the child moves freely in any direction without control and without knowledge of the limitations which society demands of him. This pattern is as unfortunate as the strict authoritarian position — perhaps even more so, since the child is never made aware of the realistic limits to which he must eventually adjust. If the parent does not present some limiting situations which can enable the child to recognize the demands being placed on him, the child cannot possibly learn to control his feelings.

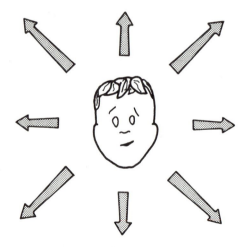

Figure 2.3

Learning is almost impossible, and the adult is inviting the child to continually test the situation in a frantic effort to determine if any rules exist.

The child is in for a rude awakening whenever he enters situations which demand rules. Unfortunately, those who finally teach this "untutored child of nature" will not do so in the comfortable understanding way of the parent.

Freedom with control

In considering discipline which is appropriate for children there is a middle ground somewhere between the extremes of "strict authority" and "sheer indulgence." Figure 2.4 illustrates our interpretation of appropriate discipline.

Here we have the original "Wall of No" but now there are openings. In life there are "No's," but in life other

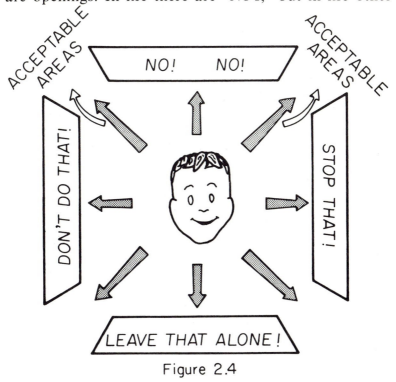

Figure 2.4

alternatives often exist. There is an absolute "No" in hitting the TV set with a mallet. There is no room for "maybe tomorrow" or "perhaps" or "hit it lightly." TV sets cost too much to allow for hammer-hitting type of experimentation. However, there are many acceptable areas where a wooden mallet can be used — on a pounding board, an old dishpan, a piece of wood.

Ideally our "Wall of No" remains firm in areas where it must remain firm; but the "Wall" disappears in areas where freedom may be permitted. Another important consideration in discipline is flexibility. Our "Wall of No" is flexible enough to make allowances for unusual situations which may arise. If bedtime is eight o'clock and special company is expected that evening, then bedtime may be moved to a later hour. Because special occasions arise, flexibility is demanded.

We might summarize *freedom with control* in the following manner:

Freedom with control — room for *Yes* and *No;* room for change — persons who love their children will discipline them. The child must learn that there are times when a *No* is useful and appropriate. In some situations a prohibition is absolute. There are times when a child needs to be told: "That sort of behavior will not be tolerated in this classroom." No individual — child or adult — can have his or her way all the time. We like to think of freedom with control as a bank account where we make many deposits of the *Yes* nature and few withdrawals of the *No* nature. When the child moves into situations outside the home and has a good *Yes* account, he can withstand the buffeting of *No* which society inevitably provides. With many outlets and many acceptable avenues of entry, the child can accept the avenues which are closed.

Freedom with control implies an understanding of the child's needs and abilities. This means we do not make demands on the child that he is unable to understand. For example, we recognize that the very young child needs to explore feelings of autonomy; to learn the feeling of "I-ness" — to learn that he is an individual in his own right. We do not expect him to understand and internalize the concept of sharing until later, when he is less egocentric and capable of understanding the concept of "we-ness." Freedom with control does not mean one capriciously indulges the child. Rather it recognizes that he is a young person learning to cope with this complex world.

Freedom with control implies learning through understanding rather than learning through fear. For parents and teachers it means making decisions on the important limits and holding to these; while permitting freedom in areas where freedom can be freely given. As adults we want to be informed on the rules and laws which affect us. The child also wishes to know the rules of his home and society.

A dilemma emerges

Following this philosophical frame of reference we felt that we had a working theory for teaching children in the home and in the classroom setting. If one provided the child with many open avenues for exploration — if one had some definite prohibitions — the child should indeed develop an understanding of self. He should also develop stability, freedom with control and a healthy realistic approach to society.

In encountering young people and adults our philosophy toward discipline appeared to prove itself. Persons who had been reared under highly strict, rigid conditions — seemed to be rigid, unimaginative and very tough. For example, we remember interviewing one father who pounded his fist on the desk and shouted: "I believe in whipping my children with a strap! They learn to behave or I beat the h_____ out of them. My daddy whipped me and I learned. . . . So I whip them." Even the studies by Sears and his associates confirmed these observations. Their studies had shown that nonaggressive children were those whose parents stopped aggression when it occurred but did not use punitive means to do so. Sears noted that while punishment might stop aggression momentarily — it often generated more hostility in the child.

Unfortunately we also interviewed a number of adults whose experiences ran counter to this theory. We interviewed happy, healthy creative adults who reported their parents had been very strict. Yet these persons seemed happy, well-adjusted and content in spite of being reared in an atmosphere of rather tight control.

On the other hand, we interviewed several adults supposedly reared under rather permissive conditions. However, these persons seemed uncertain, listless and even hostile. Then, one day, an interesting event occurred on our playground which provided us with some insight into our dilemma:

Ms. Ida Belle, noted for her permissive attitude, was in the yard with a small group of boys. The boys were playing near the gate and finally opened it. (Note: This school was adjacent to a busy street and there was a firm rule against children opening the gate and leaving the playground.) Seeing that Ms. Ida Belle did nothing about their transgression, the boys edged further out across the street. One child barely escaped being hit. Even as this event unfolded, the teacher did nothing. Suddenly the significance of this event struck us! Ms. Ida Belle was not really so permissive — she just did not care!

We could label Ms. Ida Belle's method as the "Does Nothing" approach. When following this course of action the teacher ignores children or simply neglects her duty. The approach of "Does Nothing" reflects an attitude —the adult is transmitting an emotional climate concerning discipline to the child. Sears, et al, reported similar circumstances in their parent interviews on child rearing. They noted that where mothers were often highly tolerant (or careless) in their attitude toward undesirable behavior or the punishment of that behavior; their children showed high aggressive outbursts. We felt we were observing the same phenomenon. Thus, it seemed that the control continuum was not sufficient to explain the effects of behavior and control.

In 1959, Shaefer utilized factor analysis to construct a "Hypothetical circumplex model of maternal behavior." His model suggested two dimensions for considering discipline. One dimension, "control to autonomy" is similar to the control continuum discussed here; the second dimension was labelled, "love to hostility."

This second dimension seemed to add greatly to our understanding of practical discipline as it related to home and classroom and perhaps to solve the dilemma raised in this section.

The Climate Continuum

Sears' discussion of the "tolerant, careless" mother; the observation of Ms. Ida Belle and her "Do Nothing" behavior — actually reflected an attitude toward children. These observations, coupled with Shaefer's second dimension, help us raise several questions of great significance to the adults who discipline children. These questions include: "What is the emotional climate of the situation in which I mete our control techniques?" "Is my attitude one of warmth and caring; or is my attitude one of ignoring and neglect?" "Do I transmit a feeling that I am accepting or does the child feel I am indifferent?" "Am I cooperative or antagonistic?" "Am I indulgent or indifferent?" Dunaway discusses a dramatic behavior change in the teacher and the total class when the emotional climate was altered.

Our own teaching experience and observations lead us to firmly believe that children have emotional antennae which can and do receive the feeling tones generated by the teacher. The child quickly learns to determine the emotional climate of the classroom. Since he is physically defenseless against most adults, his own survival may depend upon how well he can accurately assess this climate and its consequences.

Figure 2.5 shows the climate continuum coupled with our original control continuum. The shaded area in Figure 2.5 represents the area in which appropriate discipline can occur. This illustration represents some interesting additions and changes in thinking from the material presented in Figure 2.1.

The "acceptable" range of the control continuum has been broadened. This change recognizes that adults can range from moderately strict to moderately permissive and that children can succesfully adapt without psychological harm. In recent years the philosophy surrounding discipline has not been so generous. From the 30's to the mid-seventies, many psychologists, teachers and parents were appalled at any discipline which suggested even the slightest

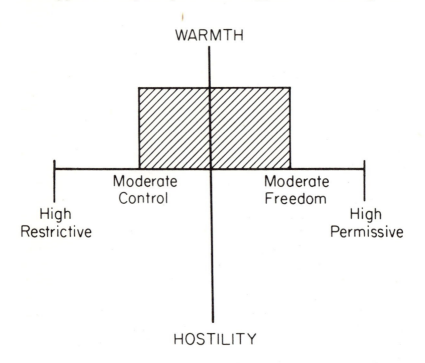

Figure 2.5

control over children. On the contrary, Figure 2.5 suggests that little or no control is unacceptable. Actually our illustration suggests that extremes in control (either high restrictive or high permissive) are inappropriate and may even be harmful to children.

The most significant variable in Figure 2.5 is the emotional climate of the home and classroom in meting out discipline. Thus, the adult should ask: "Is my discipline viewed by the child in an atmosphere of love, warmth and caring?" or "Does the child view my control as the action of a hostile, indifferent adult?"

Thus, we are suggesting that children can tolerate a reasonably wide range of control in the discipline situation. Some parents will be "pretty tough" with their children; other parents will be "pretty easy-going." Some parents will spank their children; others will not. Some teachers will keep their classes quiet and children in their seats; other teachers will tolerate a fair amount of noise and movement. It would seem that in terms of control techniques one's motto should be: "Within reason." Children are flexible and can tolerate a reasonable amount of control or a reasonable amount of freedom.

In interviewing adults we often encountered statements such as the following: "My father was really tough . . . but he loved us kids." "My mother spanked . . . but it was because she cared." "My teacher really handed out the homework. She wouldn't tolerate any monkey business . . . but I really learned math that year." "Our classroom operated at a low level of noise, a medium level of activity and a high level of love." "You wanted to succeed because the teacher wanted you to succeed." Children can learn under a reasonably wide range of conditions. Subjecting them to either extreme makes learning more difficult. The key question is not one of control — rather it is one of love and understanding.

Learning Objectives For Chapter Two:

After reading Chapter Two, "A double continuum: A new look at discipline," the reader should be able to:

1. Define and describe the control continuum in discipline.
2. Compare several discipline approaches ranging from authoritarian to indulgent and cite the effects of learning via these strategies.
3. Define and describe the emotional climate continuum.

4. Compare discipline approaches in terms of the "class-room climate" and cite the effects of learning via these strategies.
5. Identify a workable approach to discipline in terms of both child control and emotional climate.

Chapter Three

How Children Learn

Let us consider some of the ways in which behavior is learned. Most activities are the result of learned behavior — solving a puzzle, holding a paint brush, bathing a dolly, dressing oneself — all represent behaviors which are learned. Biting, hitting, pinching, and kicking are also examples of behaviors which have been learned.

The Role of Drives

We might ask a very basic question. Why do people behave at all? Early learning theorists said that behavior resulted because of basic drive reduction, and learning occurred in connection with the reduction of these basic drives. These drives were called primary or innate drives since they were basic to life itself. For example, if the individual was sufficiently hungry or thirsty, he would be forced to respond to these drives — just as a matter of mere survival. Thus the drive would impel (motivate) the person to action . . . and this action would reduce the drive.

However, in reducing the drive the individuals would learn something related to drive reduction. For example, if a person was very thirsty, he would quickly learn that water (as opposed to sand) would reduce this primary drive.

Later some psychologists discussed social drives. However, these drives were not innate; rather, they appeared to be the result of learned behavior. For example, the need for approval, praise, recognition and affection were viewed as social in nature. Like the primary drives, these social forces also moved the individual to respond.

More recently social psychologists have added exploring and curiosity as meaningful drives which can motivate. For example, in work with animals who were not thirsty or hungry there remained, nevertheless, a tendency to move about and explore. We also see this behavior in the well fed, satisfied baby. He kicks his feet, moves his head, explores his hands and generally exhibits a curious mode of behavior.

Thus we see, *a drive is created as a result of some need.* As the need increases, it creates a tension system within the individual which will finally move him to action. This tension system can be the result of a primary (innate) drive such as hunger or thirst; a secondary (learned) drive, such as the desire for recognition or approval; or an activity (curiosity) drive such as the desire for additional stimulation. This drive motivates the individual to work to reduce the tension system.

The Role of Reinforcement

It is generally believed that when a drive is reduced, learning will occur. The event or circumstance which reduces or alters the drive is termed *reinforcement.* A general rule concerning reinforcement is as follows: *Whenever a response is reinforced — there is a greater likelihood that the response will occur again.*

There are two types of reinforcement: Positive and negative. Positive reinforcements (for our purposes we can also use the term, *reward)* are pleasant stimuli such as a smile, praise, candy or attention. Whenever these events occur, the child is most likely to repeat the behavior which produced these pleasant stimuli.

In negative reinforcement an unpleasant stimulus is *removed* in order to encourage (or strengthen) a given type of behavior. Since this concept is usually difficult for teachers to grasp, let us provide an example of negative reinforcement: A child is talking to her neighbor in class and the teacher scolds the child for talking. The child will probably stop talking and the teacher will stop scolding. In this example her cessation of talking has been strengthened since the teacher stopped scolding.

Generally speaking, negative reinforcement is quicker and more effective than positive reinforcement in establishing new behaviors. However, it is almost impossible to create unpleasant situations which will provide negative reinforcers which are not, at the same time, either inherently harmful, inappropriate or very unpleasant to the child.

A third concept which is useful in our discussion is *punishment.* Many persons assume that punishments and negative reinforcements are synomous terms — however, many psychologists distinguish some subtle differences between the two concepts. Ambron (p. 151) illustrates these differences quite well with the following definitions:

> In negative reinforcement an unpleasant stimulus is *removed,* in order to *encourage* a particular response. In *punishment* an unpleasant or painful stimulus is *applied,* in order to *discourage* a given kind of behavior.

In our discussion we will refer to the concept of punishment and various forms of punishment which may be applied in order to discourage certain behaviors. For our purposes let us designate three categories of punishing behaviors: physical, verbal and ignoring. These approaches will be detailed in later sections of this chapter. However, we do wish to make several observations about the general concept of punishment and its role in changing behavior.

We recognize that punishment, particularly physical punishment, appears to work immediately and can be very effective. For example, if a child is spanked, he usually

41

stops the behavior which caused him to receive the spanking. However, this cessation of behavior may be only temporary. In many situations the child may learn ways to *avoid the punishment* — without changing the original behavior. For example, the child may wait until the teacher is not looking — or out of the room — and then repeat the behavior, because the fear of punishment has been removed.

Usually punishment, *per se,* has little meaningful long term educational value. Punishment may show that the teacher is very unhappy, but it seldom provides the child with acceptable alternatives. The teacher should recognize that in order to make the total learning experience successful, she must show the child acceptable ways of behaving — or appropriate ways to change his behavior.

We recognize that there may be instances when punishment is the only meaningful alternative. For example, a parent may punish a two year old who attempts to place a metal object in a wall receptacle. The parent may feel that a slap on the hand (with a verbal admonition of "No, No!") may be the most appropriate way to deal with this dangerous behavior. Since the two year old does not cognitively understand the dangers of electricity, physical punishment can be an effective technique — *on a short term basis.* However, it should be noted that the parent has not taught the child the inherent dangers of electricity. In the long run, this information must be ultimately communicated to the child when he can understand the concepts involved. Until that time, the adult should understand that the child has *not* learned any principles of electricity — he only recognizes that he will get his hands slapped if he touches the electrical outlet.

Positive reinforcement can generally be provided in three ways: Token reinforcement — that is giving the child a piece of candy, food, a gold star, stamps, money, a toy. Activity reinforcement — that is allowing the child the opportunity to engage in an activity of his own choosing, which he enjoys very much. Social reinforcement — that is praising the child or complimenting him or paying attention to a particular bit of behavior.

Generally token reinforcement will cause young children to respond most quickly in terms of behavior change. While token reinforcement usually works faster, it is not necessarily the most effective in the long run. As a general rule, the authors personally do not care to use token reinforcement under normal classroom conditions. It is recognized, however, that there are times when the teacher may feel a small token reinforcement is necessary to help enhance learning. In these situations, we would suggest that the tokens be used sparingly. Too often teachers fall into the "token trap." They wear smocks with kangaroo pockets and pop an M&M into each waiting mouth. At the beginning of the year the reward may be a small portion of candy. However, as the year progresses, the teacher continues to increase the rewards and "token inflation" occurs. In using tokens, the teacher should endeavor to help the child learn to work for intrinsic rewards and actually decrease the tokens over time.

Our own experience has been that children learn quite effectively via social and activity types of reinforcement and usually do not need coins or candy under regular classroom conditions. Attention, *per se,* or the opportunity to enjoy a preferred activity, are both powerful reinforcers for young children.

Undesirable behavior can be terminated in several ways: Ignoring the undesired behavior, taking away an item (removing a toy), not giving token reinforcement, removing the child from the situation (generally called, "time out"), and physical punishment. In most instances the authors have found that ignoring behavior is the best way to terminate an activity.

Classical and Operant Conditioning

Learning theorists believe there are two major forms of learning: classical and operant conditioning.

Classical Conditioning

The first studies on classical conditioning were performed on dogs by the Russian psychologist, Pavlov. When a neutral item (a bell) was rung at the same time the animal received food, an association or connection was established. After a short number of trials the animal would salivate upon hearing the bell. Under these circumstances, learning had taken place — the bell caused the dog to salivate.

This learned reflex is called a conditioned reflex . . . that is, a previously neutral item, the bell, has taken on some drive value. Or, in simpler terms, the bell motivated the dog to respond.

It is believed that much simple learning takes place in this fashion. Psychologists believe that emotional learning takes place via classical conditioning. For example, a young child may make unpleasant connections (associations) between the physician's office and receiving a shot. In some instances children are known to begin to fear all persons in offices or all persons wearing white.

Good feelings can also become associated in a similar fashion. The general good feeling one gets from viewing a lake or a sunset . . . these good feelings develop from associations made through classical conditioning.

Operant Conditioning

The concept of operant conditioning was developed by B. F. Skinner in the 1930's. One major difference between classical and operant conditioning is the sequence of the stimulus and the response. In classical conditioning the subject's response *follows* the stimulus. (In the Pavlovian experiment, the dog salivated *after* seeing the food or hearing the bell.) In operant conditioning the response *precedes* the reward. (In Skinner's experiments with pigeons, the pigeon pressed a lever and *then* he received a pellet of food.) Receiving this pellet of food is termed a *positive reinforcement* (a reward).

In a classic study Reingold, *et al,* used operant conditioning to encourage vocalizations in young infants. The experimenters rewarded random vocalizations of three month old infants by smiling and cooing. Within one week

44

there was a statistically significant increase in the vocalizations of the infants. Later, when the rewards (smiling and cooing) were terminated, the vocalizations returned to their earlier level.

Skinner's theory of reinforcement states that a person develops a certain behavior via a number of small approximations. As the skill in performing a certain behavior improves, the individual consolidates his repertoire. He retains the correct responses (which are positively reinforced) and "drops out" the incorrect responses, since they are negatively reinforced.

An example of this phenomenon can be seen by observing a child solve a wooden puzzle. The first time he attempts to put the puzzle together he makes many false moves. Since these movements do not aid in putting the puzzle together they are, in effect negatively reinforced. The movements which result in completing a portion of the puzzle are positively reinforced.

After the child has successively solved the puzzle a number of times, his movements are smooth; mistakes are fewer.

Techniques for Changing Behavior

Research shows that the teacher can effect changes in behavior by making use of the principles of reinforcement theory. Several suggestions and specific techniques are presented in this section. In most cases, if the teacher will utilize these techniques in a consistent manner and follow the specific suggestions outlined below the child will change his behavior.

1) Observe the child carefully. The value of observation cannot be overemphasized. Chapter One discussed the importance of the case study and presented some specific suggestions for observation. Prior to instituting the techniques for behavior change, observe the child's behavior in the classroom setting. We once had a child who solved all his problems by fighting. We later learned that his father had emphasized that boys who would not fight were "sissies." The father would give his son a quarter each time he "stood up and fought" for his rights. This dual combination of social and token reinforcement had its effect. The youngster soon became the class bully.

When observing a specific piece of behavior establish some baseline data. For example, let us assume you have a child who is hitting. In gathering baseline data the following questions would be helpful: Determine the frequency of the behavior, ("How many times a day does the hitting occur?") Determine the timing of the behavior. ("When does the hitting occur — throughout the day; just before lunch; early in the morning?") Determine the situations in which the hitting occurs. ("What are the circumstances under which the hitting happens — to get toys; to share; only in the block corner?") What people are involved? ("Only hits girls; will only hit specific children.")

Actually these types of baseline data are rather easy to collect. Place a sheet of paper on the wall and record the events and circumstances suggested. These data can be quite simple and to the point — for example:

9:04   Edris hit Burma. Said he wanted her trike.
10:10   Edris hit Burma at juice time. Said she was eating all the crackers.
11:42   Edris hit Burma during storytime. Said she took his book.

Our example of three items could provide the teacher with several additional questions. She might ask, "Does Edris only hit Burma?" "What happens just prior to the hitting behavior. . . . What set it off?" "Does Burma actually provoke the hitting behavior?" "Does Edris know how to share . . . how to respond in positive ways?"

As the teacher gathers additional baseline data she will be able to answer the questions of behavior frequency and determine situational variables. The writers have known teachers who gathered baseline data on several children simultaneously using this technique.

In gathering these data the teacher will also ascertain areas which are important to the child. If the teacher is to use reinforcement, she must know the child's interests sufficiently to determine areas and activities which can serve as reinforcers. Appendix B offers suggestions on constructing an "Interest Finder" chart.

2) Decide on the behavior to be changed and set up attainable goals. Ronald, age five, was a very talkative child. During discussion periods Ronald dominated the conversation, seldom allowing anyone else to talk. Initially the teacher did not set her goal to "keep Ronald quiet for ten minutes." Rather she established a goal of one minute. (Note: In changing behavior, the teacher must design success experiences which children can achieve.) Whenever Ronald met this goal during discussion period the teacher praised him. As time passed the teacher lengthened the interval before giving praise for "quiet behavior." After a few weeks Ronald (while still talkative) allowed others to share in the discussion period.

3) Reward the behavior you wish to maintain. We need to reverse our thinking patterns. Instead of waiting to pounce on bad behavior; we need to catch the child in the act of doing something good. Then, in order to maintain the "good" behavior, we reinforce it.

For example: Ms. Feldman was having trouble at juice time. Some children were neglecting to clean up. Ms. Feldman noticed that each day she was repeating the same admonitions: "Noreen, pick up your napkin . . . Desi, wipe up your spill . . . Wayne, where did you put your juice glass?"

After examining her own actions, Ms. Feldman decided to reward only the behavior she wished to maintain. She waited until the child made a correct response and said, "Noreen, thank you for putting your napkin in the waste basket . . . Desi, I see you wiped up your spill. . . . " Ms. Feldman also noticed her own attitude began to change. Instead of nagging, she found that rewarding behavior was both more effective and more satisfying. Rather than punishing children when they were deviant, she rewarded children for appropriate behavior.

Social reinforcers are usually adequate in most classroom settings. Praising a child, looking into his eyes, smiling, nodding, patting the child on the back, sitting next to the child, placing the child in your lap — these are powerful reinforcing agents. Appendix A offers many suggestions for social reinforcers.

There are also times when the teacher may wish to use an activity as a reinforcing agent. Through utilizing an interest chart (see Appendix B), the teacher can determine "natural reinforcers" — e.g., reinforcers which have a special meaning for the student.

By utilizing a social or an activity reinforcer at the appropriate time, the teacher can effectively reward the behavior she wishes to maintain.

4) Ignore the behavior you wish to discourage. Behavior which precedes a reward is strengthened. For example, Dottie, aged two, is crying. Mother gives Dottie a piece of candy and says, "That's a good girl." A few days later Dottie has a temper tantrum and again mother gives her a piece of candy to stop crying. Unknowingly the mother is reinforcing the behavior (crying) which she actually wishes to terminate. Over the long haul, the mother would do better if she ignored this behavior, thereby teaching Dottie that crying would not "pay off," e.g. be rewarded.

Ignoring can be a very powerful tool. Often the child is employing negative behavior in order to gain the attention of the adult. The act of ignoring takes away the mechanism which is being used as an attention getting device.

This suggestion is easier to state than to implement. However, most behavior can be ignored, without serious consequences. Our own experience and observation is that teachers have difficulty in being patient over a long period of time. They often expect the undesired behavior to stop the first few times it is ignored. However, if the behavior has been successful for months — or even years — it will take time before the behavior will become extinguished.

One second grade teacher, Ms. Morgan, had an entire table which continued to be noisy and disruptive. After observing Ms. Morgan over several days it was obvious that many of her approaches to this table were for the sole purpose of restoring quiet. The observer even noted that children at other tables were beginning to become involved in excessive movement, handwaving and hollering to gain the teacher's attention. One Monday Ms. Morgan announced to the class that she planned to spend her time with table groups which were quiet and prepared to utilize her services. (Note: In another section of the book we will see the value of this technique — *Clarity*. The teacher is making *clear* the rules of the situation.)

Following this announcement, Ms. Morgan would move to a table only when the children were working. In the case of the disruptive table, Ms. Morgan was particularly alert. When this table assumed an attitude of study she provided both verbal ("Now you are working quietly, that's fine.") and physical (patting a child, squeezing a hand, etc.) reinforcement.

Within a few days — by ignoring the noisy groups and involving herself with children showing performance behaviors she wished continued, the noise level of the entire class has been reduced significantly.

5) Reinforce incompatible behavior. In addition to rewarding the behavior she wishes to maintain, the adult can use the technique of rewarding incompatible behavior. In our previous example, Ms. Morgan employs this technique when she notes: "Now you are working quietly, that's fine." In this instance quiet behavior is incompatible with noisy behavior.

To use another illustration: If you wish to discourage running — ignore the running behavior but reward non-running. For example: "Martha, I am pleased to see you are walking." "Ed, I am happy to see that you are sitting at the table."

6) Recognize that some negative reinforcers and punishments may be positive!

Periodically a teacher will state that a negative reinforcer or a punishment has no effect. There are situations, however, when a reinforcing stimulus "appears" to be negative — but, in actual fact, the overall impact of the reinforcing stimulus creates a positive effect on the child.

For example, a teacher reprimands a child after he spills paint on the table. If the child spilled the paint in order to

49

get attention, the reprimand will serve as a positive reinforcement instead of a punishment. Situations can arise in the older elementary grades, middle and high school in which an older child may be "punished" by the teacher but "rewarded" by the peer group. For example, the class clown may perform an act which is annoying to the teacher. The teacher gets upset and admonishes the youngster. After class, however, the peer group may approach the child who misbehaved and say, "Hey man, that was really funny! You really bugged that old teacher!!" Thus the child may be positively reinforced when the teacher admonishes him — because he is receiving attention and praise from the peer group.

Attention *per se,* is a powerful reinforcer. Our observations show that hitting and biting often fall into this category. It is almost impossible to ignore biting behavior — thus biting is *always* noticed, *always* commented upon; often unwittingly positively reinforced.

7) Reinforcement should be immediate. An important aspect of learning, particularly with young children, is to have the reward follow closely behind the appropriate response. If the teacher has assessed correctly what is important to the child and rewards him immediately for behaviors which approximate the desired response, she will get behavior change. Unfortunately teachers often handle the situation in a haphazard fashion and are too casual in terms of praise and approval. Remember that when a child is ignored (even by accident) this ignoring can have the effect of punishment. After new behavior patterns have been established, reinforcement can be intermittent.

Timing of punishment is an important consideration. Walters, Parke and Cane (1965) theorize that the timing of discipline may be related to shame and guilt. In an experiment these authors timed their punishment in two ways: (a) just prior to playing with a forbidden item and (b) after the child had already begun to play with the item. The results of the study suggested that children punished under condition (a) were more likely to resist future temptation than the children punished under condition (b).

One possible explanation might be that early punishment aids in building superego feelings (feelings of conscience). We can observe this situation when a small child contemplates touching a forbidden object but reprimands himself saying, "No, no!"

In situations where punishment is administered "after the crime" we might theorize that the child experiences feelings of shame coupled with fear of discovery and reprisal. In the nursery school one can observe this psychological "battle" occurring within the young child. For example:

Terrance and Paul are playing in the block corner. They are building a ship to take them to the "North Pole in Alabama." Terrance reaches for a large cylinder block but Paul grabs it first. Terrance pushes Paul. Paul turns and starts to hit Terrance with the block. For a moment he stops, shakes his head and says (really to himself): "No, no." He resists striking Terrance for a few seconds — then suddenly hits him with the block. After hitting Terrance, Paul immediately scans the room to see if any adults are watching. Terrance starts to cry and says, "Bad boys hit!"

In this example of early socialization we can observe Paul feels guilt (at least pangs of conscience) as he considers whether or not he should strike Terrance. After losing this battle with the superego he becomes afraid that some adult may punish him for his transgression. Further reinforcement of these feelings of shame occur when Terrance says, "Bad boys hit!"

While it is impossible to immediately reinforce behavior on every occasion, delayed reinforcement is feasible with older children. In situations where punishment must be delayed it can still be effective if the adult talks with the child and explains the nature of the wrong doing and the proposed punishment. The adult can also help the older child learn to search for alternate solutions which can be self-regulating and yet satisfying.

8) Reinforcement is contingent upon the desired response. Suggestion seven points out the importance of timing as it is coupled with the reinforcement. Timing is crucial but, unfortunately, some adults provide positive reinforcement in anticipation of the desired response. For example the teacher may say, "I will read you a story and then we will clean up our mess." Parents easily fall into this trap — for example: "You may play now, if you will do your homework later."

Becker (1971, p. 25) refers to this problem and states: "To teach a child to carry out his responsibilities, require the less preferred activity to come before the more preferred activity." Becker refers to this postulate as *Grandma's rule:* "You do what I want you to do, before you get to do what you want to do."

Thus the teacher should employ activities which the child likes, to reinforce an activity which has less appeal to the child.

For example: "When the blocks are picked up, you may paint at the easel." "After we finish our arithmetic assignment, I have a surprise for the class."

Appendix B offers some suggestions which may help the teacher determine preferred activities for children. Grandma's rule is really the heart of contingency management. That is, after the individual has performed a specific task, he can engage in an activity that he enjoys.

For example: Carmen enjoyed working puzzles but did not like to do arithmetic problems. The teacher made an agreement with Carmen that after she solved ten problems, she could work one puzzle. Carmen began to happily work on the arithmetic, knowing that later she could play with a puzzle. Most children are willing to work for the privilege of later engaging in a preferred activity.

9) Reinforcement, initially, should be continuous. Let us discuss the nature of continuous and intermittent reinforcement. In establishing behavior change, the reinforcement must be continuous. Unfortunately teachers are often too casual when they are endeavoring to establish behavior change. If the teacher decides to reward a specific behavior, she must initially do it continuously if the change is to take place.

Example: A nursery school teacher is trying to encourage Randy to use fingerpaint. Randy gingerly places one finger in the paint. T: "Isn't that fun?" (Randy smiles faintly.) T: "Here try the paint" (shows paper). Randy tentatively touches the paint on the paper. At this moment the teacher gets distracted and moves across the room to converse with the assistant. Randy, meantime, makes a wide sweeping movement with his finger and succeeds in painting a lovely red streak across the paper. Randy looks up, smiles and hollers: "Teacher, look!" The teacher remains involved with her assistant. Randy looks at his finger, frowns and retreats to the bathroom and washes his hands. About ten minutes later the teacher returns to Randy; invites him to fingerpaint — he refuses. Unless reinforcement is continuous, it is difficult to effect change. Once the behavior is established, however, reinforcement can be intermittent and the new behavior will maintain itself.

Please note that the reverse holds true. Thus, if you wish to stop an undesired piece of behavior, punishment or negative reinforcers must likewise be continuous. If the stimuli are presented in a haphazard and unpredictable fashion, the undesired behavior will still maintain itself and change will not take place. This situation can occur when the adult "holds firm" most of the time; but occasionally "gives in" or "ignores" the misbehavior.

Example: Janice always runs in the school hallway. We observe that Janice is periodically reprimanded for running; however, this behavior is generally ignored by the teacher. We predict that Janice will continue running (which she obviously enjoys — it is a highly positive experience for her) since the overall reinforcement pattern is positive. We are correct in our prediction.

10) Reinforcement should be consistent. One of the most difficult tasks in supervision is to get beginning teachers to be consistent. Consistency is usually a big problem with parents. One can accidently create bad habits in children by alternating between "being firm" and "giving in." When teachers or parents are inconsistent, learning appropriate behavior is difficult. It is like having the rules of a game constantly changed. Generally parents and teachers are inconsistent in areas where they themselves are uncertain. This uncertainty is transferred to the child.

The best example of inconsistency the writers remember occurred in a children's summer camp. Harold, the counselor for the eleven year old boys, was experiencing difficulty in getting his campers to bed. One night one of our observers recorded the following:

Harold *(shouting)* "All right, you guys — this is the third time I am going to say, 'This is the last time to get to bed!' "
The boys continued their rough housing. Four minutes pass.

Harold *(shouting)* "All right, you guys, — I *really* mean it this time . . . this is the *fourth* time I am going to say, 'This is the *last time* to get to bed!' "
Several minutes pass. The boys engage in a pillow fight. Bill hits Irv over the head and Irv starts to cry. Harold goes over to comfort Irv.

Harold *(shouting)* "All right, you guys. . . . See what happens when you fight! Now this is the *fifth* time I am going to say, 'This is the *last time* to get to bed.' " This pronouncement is greeted with hooting and yelling.

The next day the writer overheard two of the campers in a discussion. One said, "I will bet you a candy bar that tonight Harold will say, 'This is the *tenth time* . . .'. "The other camper responded, "It's a bet!"

Please note that the campers are learning quite well. Unfortunately, they are not learning the rules which concern bedtime. Rather they have learned that rough housing, fighting and shouting types of behavior delay the unpleasant process of going to bed. By creating disturbances they are able to stay up later each evening. In addition, "bugging the counselor" becomes a rewarding experience — as the campers see they can completely confound this representative of the adult world.

11) Re-observe the child and evaluate goals. Once you set your goals for a child and decide on the behaviors you wish to reinforce, keep a record. Each day the teacher should study her observational materials to determine if her reinforcements are meeting the criteria set forth in this chapter. For example: Are the reinforcements appropriate for the particular child or group you are attempting to modify? Are the reinforcements clear, consistent and appropriately timed? Under what conditions do the reinforcements take place? How do the children respond? Based on this new information, what changes should be made in teaching strategies? Only in this manner can the teacher determine if she is meeting her goals and effecting a change in behavior.

Implementing Reinforcement Theory:

Case #1. Charlie. Several years ago a friend was teaching in a ghetto area. She had a five year old boy who was extremely quiet and withdrawn. After observing him for several days the teacher noticed the child arrived earlier than the other pupils. Her initial observations follow:

T: "Good morning Charlie."
Charlie: (no reply)
T: "How are you this morning?"
Charlie: (looks non-committal at T.)

Each morning the conversation followed a similar pattern. The teacher would comment on the weather. Charlie's clothing, plans for the day — but no topic seemed to interest the youngster. Learning that Charlie had a dog, the teacher was able to use this knowledge as the following exchange shows:

T: "Good morning Charlie."
Charlie: *(nothing)*
T: "How is your dog this morning?"
Charlie: (faint smile, shrugs shoulders)
T: "I don't believe I know your dog's name."

55

Charlie: "Ringo."

T: "Ringo, Hey, that's a great name for a dog. I'll bet you are good friends."

Through rewarding his comments and showing a genuine interest the teacher helped Charlie to talk more. As the conversation increased the teacher was able to discover other areas of interest. By mid-year, Charlie was able to converse better and share with others.

Case #2. Christopher. Ms. Markette, fourth grade teacher, noticed that Christopher had great difficulty in finishing his work. He seemed to wander around the room generally disrupting class. Ms. Markette was unable to find anything which would hold Christopher's attention for more than a few minutes.

One day during the outdoor play period, Christopher led the first grade boys in kickball. He taught the boys the rules and generally assumed a leadership role in the game. It was apparent that everyone was having a good time.

Upon returning indoors, Ms. Markette received a note from the kindergarten teacher requesting some temporary help for her class. Remembering the outside events, Ms. Markette sent Christopher to help in the kindergarten. Thirty minutes later Christopher returned to the room —all smiles. When questioned he said he would like to help again stating, "Teaching those little kids is a lot of fun!"

On the following day Christopher began to disturb the class. Ms. Markette said, "Christopher, if you can sit quietly at your seat and complete your work, I will let you help in the kindergarten." (Note that the teacher is utilizing suggestion number eight, Grandma's rule: e.g., the reinforcement is contingent upon the desired response.)

Over the next few weeks Christopher was rewarded for work behavior. In the meantime the kindergarten teacher reported that he was a great help and well liked by the kindergarten children. She, too, praised Christopher for his efforts. As time progressed, Christopher attended more to his work and wandering aimlessly about the room almost completely stopped.

Case #3. Debra. Debra talked so loudly her voice reverberated down the hall. Her loud voice carried easily and disturbed the reading groups. After determining the problem was not physiological and that hearing acuity was in the normal range, her first grade teacher devised the following strategy.

The teacher told Debra that her voice was too loud and was disturbing others. Using a TV set as an analogy, the teacher explained that Debra needed to "turn down the volume." The teacher added: "To remind you, I will 'pretend' to turn the volume down on your voice." The teacher then gave a visual demonstration of turning down a volume knob. Debra laughed and said, "Oh! I see! Whenever you turn you hand I will lower my voice."

Later in class when Debra's voice became loud, the teacher would give Debra a visual cue. In addition, when Debra did talk in a quiet voice, the teacher would nod and smile. Within two weeks Debra was speaking in a normal voice.

Case #4. Sam. One year a teacher friend approached the authors concerning one of her four year old pupils. Following Suggestion #1 we observed the child (Sam) for one week to establish baseline data. We found several interesting things:

1) Sam bit or hit someone an average of 23 times a day!

2) It was obvious that the hitting behavior was highly rewarding. Other classmates quickly gave in to Sam's demands — if he wanted an item — he got it.

3) In many instances (as one would suspect) when Sam approached other children they would run away.

4) The teachers were often inconsistent whenever Sam bit or hit another child. At different times during the week the teachers had ignored Sam, physically retrained him, argued with him, threatened him, removed him from the situation.

5) Observation also indicated that most of the adult contacts (the teacher and two assistants) were negative in nature — restraining Sam, reproaching Sam, etc. During this period we observed an interesting incident. One of the

57

assistant teachers was playing Looby Loo with the children. Our observation is as follows:

T: "Here we go Looby-Loo. . . . Sam, hold Darlene's hand. . . . Here we go Looby-Lie. . . . Sam, will you leave Mary alone. . . . Here we go Looby-Lie. . . . Sam, will you leave Mary alone. . . . Here we go Looby — SAM STOP! — Loo. . . . "

Sadly, the assistant had nothing positive to say to Sam and we observed nineteen prohibitions during this single situation! Clearly this circumstance, coupled with Sam's biting behavior, demanded action.

After much discussion several decisions were made. 1) We would use a "time out" technique and remove Sam to a nearby room. 2) Whenever Sam bit a child the teacher would say in a definite but firm voice that the behavior was inappropriate and would not be allowed to continue. 3) The teacher would remove Sam from the room as expeditiously (and as matter-of-factly) as possible. In other words we did not want the teacher to engage in a fight or argument with Sam — rather to clearly and consistently point out the misbehavior and remove him from the room. 4) The teacher would place Sam in the "time out" room saying, "When you can calm down and play with other children, you may return to the group." (Note: The "time out" room was a well lighted store room, sixteen feet square. The room was cleared of most of the boxes and two small chairs were placed in the room. There was a small window in the door.) It was agreed that if, at any time, Sam was frightened or did not calm down in four minutes the teacher would enter the room, comfort and calm him. It was also agreed that initially, because of Sam's volatile behavior, if he was calm for ten seconds, the teacher would open the door, smile and compliment Sam on this calm, quiet behavior and announce that he could return to the room. 5) A complete record would be kept of Sam's hitting and biting behavior including type and time the behavior occurred, the circumstance, and the amount of time spent in the "time out" room. (Note: The longest

Sam ever stayed in the time out room was two minutes: 34 seconds.) Figure 3.1 shows a complete record of the biting and hitting behavior.

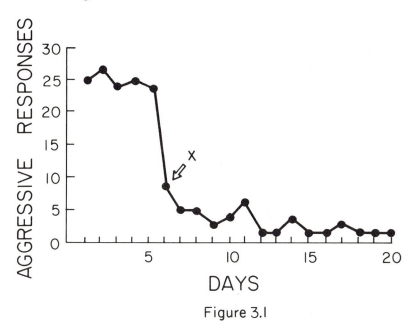

Figure 3.1

Figure 3.1 shows that during the week when baseline data were obtained, Sam averaged 23 aggressive responses per day! On the first day the "time out" procedure was employed, Sam's biting and hitting dropped to an N = 8 times. (Denoted as "x" on the graph.) Figure 3.1 shows the number of aggressive responses continued to decline during the ensuing weeks. By the fourth week the biting had stopped and the hitting behavior had declined to one or two transgressions per day.

In addition to utilizing the time out technique, we worked with the teachers in an effort to determine areas where Sam could be positively reinforced for appropriate behavior. One of Sam's favorite activities was playing in the sandbox. The teachers took special pains to pay attention to Sam and comment that he could play

59

successfully without resorting to biting or hitting. During the first week, through intensive observation, the teachers were able to discover several other activities which Sam enjoyed and to reward him whenever appropriate behavior occurred. The teachers also began to ascertain "potential problem situations" and moved to redirect Sam before a problem arose. Whenever possible, the teachers tried to anticipate Sam's behavior and give him a warning *prior* to a hitting or biting episode. As Figure 3.1 shows, the biting and hitting behavior lessened significantly over time. Coupled with this decrease, Sam began to develop more appropriate social responses.

During this period Sam also began receiving positive reinforcements from some of his classmates. As the hitting and biting diminished, several children became friendly with Sam and actively sought him as a playmate. Interestingly, however, we felt the biggest change had occurred with the adults in the group. As they observed positive reinforcement working effectively, they became more conscious of their contacts with other children.

Reinforcement is not a panacea; it will not solve all behavior problems. Reinforcement is one way in which children learn; it is an effective tool when used wisely by the teacher. Understanding the principles of reinforcement will help the teacher in modifying behavior. However, children also learn via other methods. This book will explore these alternate methods of learning and their effect on the way children behave. In the next section of this chapter we will discover that children can learn strategies of behaving through observation.

Modeling Behavior

For years people have noted that children often imitate their parents. It was probably like these observations which lead to the old adage, "Like father, like son." We can observe modeling behavior in a two year old as he assumes the same physical stance as his father — shifting his feet, folding his arms, cocking his head in similar fashion. The authors remember watching a ten month old baby babbling in a strong husky voice for several minutes. Then the baby picked up a Teddy Bear. Holding the bear close to his body, the infant immediately changed his babbling pattern of speech to a quiet, cooing mode — actually duplicating some of the inflections of his mother.

Psychologists use the terms imitative or modeling behavior to describe these events. Freud pointed out the powerful role of the parent in child rearing and noted that the child often imitated one of his parents. Later John Watson, the behavioral psychologist, made similar observations. Since behavior was copied by the child, Watson offered some highly specific suggestions on ways in which parents should behave in rearing their children. In the 40's Dollard and Miller theorized that parental nurturance was the guiding factor in the child's imitation of his parents. Thus, as the mother satisfied the child's basic needs, she became a reinforcing agent. Actually in the theory postulated by Dollard and Miller the parent became a "reinforcing attribute." Or — to use our earlier terminology: Originally the parent was a "neutral cue." However, since the parent was in the vicinity of the reinforcement, the parent itself, acquired drive value. As the child associated this nurturing adult with the reduction of the drive, he began to imitate the parent — and this imitative behavior became rewarding in and of itself.

However, children do not limit imitative behavior exclusively to their parents. Lewin and his students once did a study on group leadership. They used three types of leaders: democratic, autocratic and laissez-faire. They found that the type of leadership employed influenced the behavior of the entire group. Children began to imitate their leader and responded in ways appropriate to the climate the leader created. In the autocratic group, the children were often harsh with each other; in the democratic group, the children worked together in a spirit of cooperation. Interestingly, this modeling continued when the leader was not present in the room. The autocratic group became unruly and tyrannical when the leader was absent. The democratic group, on the other hand, continued much in the same spirit as when the leader was present. This research suggests some interesting questions for teachers. What type of leadership role does the teacher assume? How do children react to this role? What kind of classroom climate does the teacher create and how does this affect children.

Recently Bandura and his associates have carried on a number of studies and extended our knowledge in the area of modeling. Their research is usually referred to as social learning theory. Based on this research the writers would make two general observations:

1) Children often model their behavior after the adult who teaches them. Children do learn through imitation! This observation is very important to the teacher and the parent. It means that children closely observe the adult and utilize her mode of behavior as a "model" for their own interactions. Please note the rule does not say: Children model the teacher's *good* behavior or *outstanding* behavior . . . the statement refers to *all* behavior.

— On the days we holler: children learn.
— On the days we are unfair: children learn.
— On the days we tell children that we value individual differences . . . and then treat all children alike: children learn.

A noisy teacher not only contributes to the noisy classroom; she often creates the situation. Thus the child may ignore what is verbalized but imitate the actions of the teacher. The next time your classroom becomes unusually noisy — do not comment on the noise. Lower your own voice and speak clearly, but quietly. Usually, under these circumstances, the children will do likewise and the entire room will become quieter. The child views the teacher as a reinforcing property, per se, and imitates her behavior. Children will imitate the teacher's voice; her social overtures to others; her attitudes and even her mannerisms.

Several studies have found a high correlation between punitive parents and aggressiveness on the part of the child. Once a father said to the writers, "I don't know why

George hits . . . because everytime he hits somebody I hit him!!" Obviously the child was modeling his behavior after his father. Studies also suggest that where parents lack sufficient self-control, the child often lacks self-control.

2) Children model behavior they observe as being rewarded. This is an important point for teachers. Earlier we observed that under certain conditions some negative reinforcers or acts of punishment could, in fact, be perceived as positive reinforcement.

Mary sees Adam hit Joey and takes his car. Later she observes Adam knock down some block towers and gleefully kick the blocks all over the room. She watches Adam take Hilda's place at the easel, forcing Hilda to go elsewhere. For all these wonderful feelings of power and dominance Mary also observes that the teacher merely says, "Adam, we share here." At storytime, after a series of misbehaviors the teacher says, "Adam, you must sit in my lap for awhile and calm down." In Mary's eyes, Adam has been beautifully rewarded for kicking, hitting and generally dominating others.

Bandura and his associates have also found that children learn from a vicarious model, e.g., a character on TV or in the movies. Children model behavior which they see rewarded. Thus, even though the "bad guy" on television receives his punishment in the last 30 seconds of an episode, children may still imitate the earlier behaviors of the perpetrator. For example: The "bad guy" gets his way by hitting or killing; he obtains a new car by stealing; he avoids pain by lying; he makes fun of others by ridicule; he gets rich by cheating. Research suggests the child may learn more (be more influenced) by the large number of intermittent rewards and lose sight of the final punishment meted out just prior to the closing commercial.

The research on modeling does suggest that children indeed model their behavior after the adult who teaches them. Recently a teacher friend related the following observation to the authors. She said, "I have been teaching fourth grade in the same school for five years. There are

63

two other fourth grade teachers and we all started in this school at the same time. This fall it finally dawned on me that classrooms do take on the personality of the teachers.

Ms. Rutherford is a quiet calm teacher. She is rather strict and her classes are always the quietest of the three of us. Ms. Redmond is noisy and rather frenetic. Her class is always the loudest and the children always seem to be at 'loose ends.' She screams at them and they scream back. And, you know, in spite of the different children each year, it is amazing how the general Gestalt remains the same."

Learning Objectives For Chapter Three:

After reading Chapter Three, "How children learn," the reader should be able to:

1. Have an overview of the ways in which learning occurs.
2. Understand the role of drives in motivating behavior.
3. List ways to effect behavior change.
4. Discuss the importance of timing in discipline.
5. Given a problem in discipline, the reader should be able to:
    a. design strategies to maintain desirable behavior.
    b. decide the behavior to be changed and set up attainable goals.
6. Discuss the importance of the teacher as a model and the effect of modeling behavior in discipline.
7. Discuss the role of reward and punishment and how it effects behavior change.
8. Define the following terms:
    a. drive
    b. social drive
    c. classical conditioning
    d. operant conditioning
        — positive
        — negative
        — token

e. reinforcement (types)
   — positive
   — negative
   — token
   — activity
   — social
f. incompatible behavior
g. modeling behavior

Chapter Four

Two Research Designs
That Really Help Teachers

A few years ago at The Merrill-Palmer Institute in Detroit, Sigel and his associates did several studies on discipline. About the same time, at nearby Wayne State University, Kounin and his colleagues were conducting studies in the same general area. However, each group approached the subject matter from different vantage points — yet both have some practical implications for the teacher.

The Sigel Paradigm

Sigel and his associates became interested in the type of techniques a teacher used to influence the behavior of a child. They found the teacher had, in her repertoire, a number of influence techniques (IT) available to her at any given moment. These researchers studied the type of influence techniques used by teachers and their subsequent effectiveness on the child. (NOTE: The child who receives the IT is sometimes labelled the "target child.") Thus, these researchers studied the types of IT used by teachers and their subsequent effectiveness on the target child. The Sigel paradigm is presented in Figure 4.1:

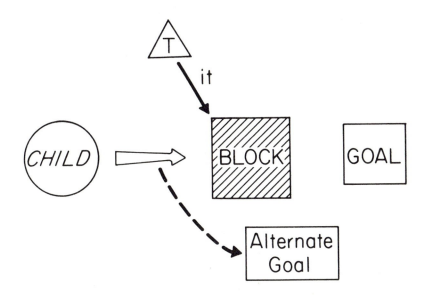

Figure 4.1

To explain this design, let us use an example: Johnny is headed toward a doll which is currently being used by Fan. The teacher (indicated by the triangle) sees a potential conflict and decides to change (influence) Johnny's behavior (use an IT). In our example the teacher would say, "Johnny, Fan is playing with that doll. Here is one you may play with." Johnny accepts the proffered doll (the alternate goal). Utilizing this design, Sigel's group made several interesting observations which are helpful to the teacher.

1. If the influence technique is clear, the child is more likely to comply with the teacher's IT.

This observation appears to be so simple. That is, if the teacher clearly states a rule — or a reason — there is a greater likelihood that the child will positively respond to the teacher's wishes. While teachers and parents recognize this observation, it is amazing how often it is ignored. Generally adults use desist techniques which do not clarify rules or standards — nor do they provide any corrective help or information. In most cases the adult is remarkably unclear and shouts, "Quit" or "Stop that" or "That's enough!" After presenting unclear directions or fuzzy reasons, the adult then expects the child to somehow miraculously comply. Interestingly, most studies dealing with discipline show that the teacher focuses on stopping behavior; she does not show the child legal acceptable behavior.

2. If the influence technique is consistent, the child is more likely to comply.

In Chapter Three, the importance of consistency was discussed as a major factor in reinforcement. In his research, Sigel also found this element of consistency to be extremely important. Quite simply stated, learning is much easier when the learning conditions remain constant. If children are to learn rules of behaving, the teacher must be consistent. Unfortunately, when the teacher is inconsistent, the net result is that the child begins to test the teacher — to discover the outer limits of the rules or to test the teacher's patience.

The following observation from a first grade setting illustrates inconsistent behavior on the part of the teacher:

Ms. Roberts is with the Bluebirds reading group. Frank and Bob are doing seatwork. Frank says something to Bob.

Ms. Roberts: "Alright boys — stop." (The boys ignore Ms. Roberts and continue to talk . . . two minutes pass.)

Ms. Roberts: "Boys, shhh!"

The boys disregard the teacher's comments and continue to talk. One of the Bluebirds (Etta) says, "Ms. Roberts, I can't hear."

Ms. Roberts *(Loud voice):* "Alright, boys!!!" The boys continue to talk.

Ms. Roberts *(Loud voice):* "Frank, if you and Bob do not stop, I am going to separate you."

The boys stop talking. They are quiet for nearly a minute and then commence talking again.

Ms. Roberts *(Looks at boys, frowns):* "Don't forget, I warned you!"

Etta: "Ms. Roberts, I can't hear."

Ms. Roberts: "Just ignore them, Etta; they will get quiet in a minute."

In our example it is quite clear that Frank and Bob have learned that the teacher does not carry out her admonitions. Therefore, they have learned to ignore her statements. We can observe similar inconsistent behavior on the part of the mother of a three year old.

C: "Mother, can I go outside?"

M: "No, not now." *(Mother is busy in the kitchen.)*

C: "Mother, Please — Please, let me go out!"

M: "No, hush, I am busy."

C: *(Pulls on mother's skirt)* "Please! Please! Pretty please!!!"

M: *(Somewhat exasperated)* "Will you be quiet! I am trying to cook. . . . You are *not* going outside!! . . . and *that is final!"*

C: *(Whining)* "I want to play. I want to go out!!"

M: *(Shakes head)*

C: *(Hits mother on leg)* Out!! Out!!"

M: "In a few minutes you can go out. Now, hush!"

C: *(Hits mother on leg)* "Out!!"

M: *(Ignores hitting; continues working)*

C: *(Whining and stamping feet)* "I want to go out now!! Pretty please with sugar on it!"

M: "Well, since you said it nicely, I guess you can go out."

The child in our example has learned quite well.

Mother's inconsistency has taught the child that if he is persistent for a long period of time, the rules will change.

3. If the influence technique offers the child an alternative, the child is more likely to comply.

Several years ago we conducted an informal study with a group of trained teachers and confirmed Sigel's observation. Teachers who offered children alternative solutions — or who redirected children to alternate goals — were more successful in terms of influencing behavior. Unfortunately, we observed that teachers usually appeared too busy or too preoccupied to offer alternative approaches. Children were told that some action was prohibited — but were not provided any avenues toward acceptable behavior. (Please note that these teachers paid dearly for these transgressions — since we found they were less successful in terms of behavior management.)

Some examples may be useful:

Instead of: "Leave Mary's doll alone!"
  Try: "There *(point)* is a doll you can play with."

Instead of: "Stop that!"
  Try: "I wonder if you could discover another way we could. . . . "

Instead of: "Don't throw those blocks. . . . "
  Try: "Let's get the bean bags and. . . . "

4. If the influence technique informs the child of future consequences, the child is more likely to comply.

Another influence technique, similar in character to an alternate goal, is to provide the child with a warning. In this manner the child becomes prepared for some future action or consequence. Most teachers have learned that children are more likely to comply with a suggestion, if they are advised of the action beforehand. Some examples will illustrate this point:

Instead of: "Marty, we are going outside."
   Try: "Marty, in five minutes it will be time to go outside."

Instead of: "Jane, pick up those blocks!"
   Try: "Jane, when you finish building, remember to pick up the blocks."

In essence the warning provides the child with a psychological "set" (or predisposition) of a future consequence or action which will be taken. It is important to remember that once the "set" has been given, the teacher should follow through with the stated action at the appropriate time.

5. If the influence technique "reflects feelings," the child may respond in kind.

A commonly used control technique is to reflect the child's feelings. While this strategy may convey empathy to the child, the discipline studies suggest that this approach may also have unusual repercussions. In observing the child's reactions to reflective influence techniques, it was observed that the child often became more upset. For example, when the teacher used statements like, "You really are angry, aren't you?" or "I can understand that you feel like hitting." It was observed that children often continued to hit or became even more angry than before.

Such observations suggest that the adult should carefully choose situations in which reflective techniques would be appropriate. It is quite possible that reflective techniques may actually contribute to the disturbance rather than having a calming effect.

6. The intensity of an influence technique has little relation to compliance.

Some teachers and parents feel that loud or rough talking will aid in compliance. The earlier example of Ms. Roberts illustrates that intensity has little relationship to the effectivenes of the influence technique. Sigel's associates found that of all the influence techniques available to the adult, "sheer power" was the *least effective* technique available to gain compliance.

In their study, they reported that "sheer power" was effective only about fifty percent of the time. Thus, if Sigel is correct, consider the following example:

T: "Okay, Lillie, I am really mad. . . . You cannot do that!! You will not hit!!! I really mean you will stay right here. . . . You absolutely can not hit Diane!"

Given the example above . . . if the research finding is valid, about fifty percent of the time the child will still misbehave. And this misbehavior will occur in spite of the teacher's use of "sheer power" and absolute authority.

7. If the influence technique provides a "cushion," the child is more likely to comply.

The term, "cushion," is used to describe a means by which the influence technique can be softened or made more palatable. Research shows that when the teacher employs a "cushion," her chances of success dramatically improve. Even if she employs sheer power, her chances will be greater if she adds a cushion. Unfortunately, research also shows that most teachers do not utilize this technique. Osborn (1962) found eighty-nine percent of the time teachers employed a desist technique without any cushion.

Some examples of influence techniques are presented coupled with a cushion:

Instead of: "Everybody clean up!"
    Try: "In three minutes we will have to stop and clean up." (Influence technique coupled with a "warning cushion.")

Instead of: "Leave that drill alone!"
    Try: "Jerri, the drill can be dangerous. Please wait until I can help you." (Influence technique cushioned with reasoning.)

72

Instead of: "That is Abbey's puzzle."
   Try: "Burt, Abbey is playing with that puzzle. You may work with one of these." (Influence technique cushioned with an alternative.)

Instead of: "Shut your mouth!"
   Try: "Noreen, you must be quiet now. After Simon speaks, you may have your turn."

Note: In this last illustration the "sheer power" technique has been softened in volume and intent. Nevertheless, the technique remains clear and definite and yet offers the child an avenue for appropriate behavior.

The Kounin Paradigm

Kounin and his associates became interested in the "ripple effect" of discipline. The ripple effect is the effect a control technique exerts — not on the target child — but on the other children in the classroom as the technique "ripples out" from the target child. The Kounin paradigm can be presented as follows:

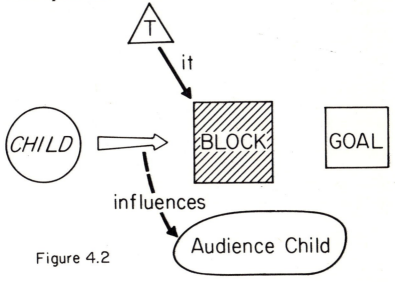

Figure 4.2

73

To explain Figure 4.2, let us use an example:

Ruth is using counting blocks in math. She knocks the blocks on the floor. The teacher admonishes Ruth for her carelessness. In the Kounin research the following questions would be raised: In correcting Ruth, what effect does the IT have on the child (the audience) sitting nearby? Does the type of technique employed make any difference to the audience child? Does the intensity of the IT have any effect?

The researchers found that the IT not only had an effect on the target child — it had an effect on the audience child as well. In other words, discipline does have a ripple effect. Children in the classroom learn by observing the discipline meted out to others.

Kounin's associates report several significant findings which have meaning for teachers.

1. When the influence technique is clear, the audience children respond with increased comformance.

This finding is quite similar to Sigel's results with the target child. Kounin also found that when the control technique lacked clarity, the audience children responded with more non-conformity.

This suggestion seems so obvious. If the teacher is clear on meting out her discipline, there is a greater likelihood that both the target child and the audience will improve in conformity. However, Ofchus (1960) found that 92 percent of the time teachers gave no reason why misbehavior was bad. In 96 percent of the cases the teacher did not clarify rules or group standards. Ofchus found that, in most instances, the teacher provided no clarity and little information beyond, "I will punish you in some fashion." We would suggest the following:

Instead of: "Shh! Shh!"
    Try: "Brenda would you please speak softly so you won't disturb the rest of the class."

74

Instead of: "Henry, quit!"
Try: "Henry, you cannot hit Timmy."

Please note that in the last example presented the teacher could also increase the effectiveness of her control if she provided an alternative for the child.

2. When an influence technique is firm, the audience children respond with increased conformance.

The authors' own observations would suggest that this finding applies to the target child as well as the audience children.

Firmness is an interesting ingredient in discipline. It carries a degree of comfort for the child in the sense that the child usually translates firmness into knowing. Whenever a teacher is firm, a noticeable degree of assuredness accompanies this technique. Usually children are aware of this quality and conform to the teacher's IT.

One of the most difficult tasks in teacher education is to teach students how to be firm in their discipline. Students sometimes lack the "courage of their convictions" and this uncertainty is reflected in a lack of firmness. Classroom management does require rules. While rules should ideally be derived from democratic discussion, there are instances where this method is clearly inappropriate. The teacher must make a decision and carry it out with clarity and firmness.

Beginning teachers usually reflect their uncertainty by their general demeanor and manner in which they handle a discipline problem. If a particular child is difficult to manage, a beginning teacher will "ignore" misbehavior and hope the situation will magically resolve itself. Unfortunately, both the target child and the audience children learn that the teacher vascillates and is uncertain. This lack of firmness leads children to test limits.

One can also observe uncertainty in a teacher's voice. For example: "Judy, don't you think you should share your toys?" This statement lacks firmness and clarity and

75

reflects the techer's indecisiveness. The absence of a firm commitment actually invites non-compliance. .

Instead of: "Willard, you really don't want to hit Annie, do you?"
      Try: "Willard, I will not permit you to hit Annie. "

Instead of: "Class don't you think we could all hear better if we just decided to get quiet?"
      Try: "Before we continue, the class must get quiet. "

(NOTE: If only two or three children are talking, the teacher will improve her influence technique by addressing these children by name. For example: "Lane, before we continue, I want you and Troyce Anne to quit talking.")

3. When an influence technique is rough, the audience children become upset.

Kounin's term "rough control technique" is the equivalent of Sigel's "sheer power" technique. Interestingly, both researchers found that this technique actually did little in controlling behavior. As mentioned earlier, Sigel found "sheer power" to be effective only about fifty percent of the time.

Kounin found (1970, p. 54), "When teachers stopped a misbehavior with roughness (anger and/or punitiveness, but mostly anger) the audience pupils reacted with more behavior disruption (overt signs of apprehension or anxiety, less involvement in the ongoing task) than when teachers desisted without roughness . . . children with punitive teachers manifested more conflict about classroom behavior, were less concerned about school matters and more preoccupied with aggression. . . . One might point out that punitiveness related not only to misbehavior and desist events, but was a general teacher mode of behavior that was applied to other issues, such as making mistakes in work."

The problem of highly intense control techniques has been beautifully summarized by Kounin and Gump (1957, p. 160): "Roughness did not lead to increased conformance and decreased nonconformance. Instead rough techniques were followed by an increase in behavior disruption. *Severe techniques did not make for 'better' behavior in the child. Severe techniques merely upset him."*

Summary

The two research projects by Sigel and by Kounin have some practical implications for the parent and teacher.

Suggestions for the teacher include:
— Recognizing the importance of consistency.
— Recognizing the importance of clarity.
— Informing the child of future consequences.
— Recognizing the difference between firmness and roughness.
— Recognizing that the "power" of a technique has little to do with conformity.
— Recognizing the importance of providing a "cushion"
- provide a reason
- provide a warning
- provide an alternative
- soften the intent of the IT

The Teacher should be aware that when she disciplines the "target child" the effect of the IT will "ripple out" to the rest of the children in the classroom.

Finally, and perhaps the most important . . . remember to offer children "a way out." That is, show the child why the behavior is unacceptable and then provide him with a workable alternative. There should be an educational quality to discipline. While an influence technique may show the child that certain behavior is forbidden, the teacher should also provide the child with ways to change and to improve his behavior.

Learning Objectives For Chapter Four:

After reading Chapter Four, "Two research designs that really help teachers," the reader should be able to:

1. Identify influence (discipline) techniques which will be most successful in a classroom setting.
2. Differentiate between firmness and roughness in administering discipline.
3. Differentiate between a "power technique" and a "cushion technique" and discuss the relative value of the technique chosen.
4. Compare techniques with clarity and consistency and discuss the relative value of the techniques chosen.
5. Identify the research paradigms utilized in the chapter and compare the ways in which the designs are alike and different.
6. Define the following terms:
   a. influence technique
   b. target child
   c. audience child
   d. clarity
   e. consistency
   f. firmness
   g. alternate goal
   h. warning cushion
   i. reason cushion
   j. ripple effect
   k. sheer power

Chapter Five

Drugs: A Special Problem

Drugs are everywhere. Many of the drugs we use are perfectly legal; they are used daily and can serve many good purposes. Some drugs have a medicinal value and may help the individual for whom they were perscribed. Nose drops, eye drops and drugs like tobacco, aspirin, coffee and alcohol may be seen as reasonably harmless. Unfortunately, a large number of persons misuse these and a host of other drugs.

Until recently drugs were relatively unknown in the public schools. In the 40s and 50s, a youngster might smoke a cigarette in the school restroom — or a high school student might "sneak" a half-pint of gin into the punch bowl of the junior-senior prom. Most students were as innocent as the youngsters depicted on the television program, "Happy Days."

Unfortunately events in the late 60s and early 70s caused changes in our attitudes and behavior. In the process the children of America lost their innocence. College kids were encouraged to "drop out" and "turn on." LSD, alcohol, marijuana and angel dust became common on the college scene. Fraternities began to have "fruit salad" parties where participants all brought a variety of pills and made a "salad" which was guaranteed to give you a "high" or make you sick.

To-day there is an epidemic among children in the United States. Like the plagues of the Middle Ages, this epidemic may wipe out nearly a total generation . . . however, this epidemic will not kill — rather it will harm our children psychologically by killing ambition and the desire to succeed. It will dull their conscious awareness and lull them into a false feeling of well-being. For many children it will cause them to commit burglaries and thefts and become involved in illicit sex. This epidemic will also harm our children physically by causing brain damage, liver and lung ailments. When they become adults their own children may be born with birth defects as a result of drugs.

Incidence of Drug Abuse

Many teachers and parents have failed to realize the extent of the drug problem. Recently the authors were giving a lecture in a small community in one of our southeastern states. In casual conversation several teachers and parents commented, "We really do not have a drug problem in our little city. We have a few high school kids who get drunk . . . and we may have some alcohol abuse . . . but very few of our students ever see marijuana or any of the hard drugs."

The next day we interviewed a couple of high school students in that same community. The following comments are excerpted from that interview:

> I don't see how some of our parents and teachers can be so stupid! We have drugs everywhere. I can get on the telephone and have speed, quaaludes, angel dust or cocaine delivered here in fifteen minutes. . . . We used to smoke pot on the school bus, but the driver recognized the smell and made us stop. Now we just roll joints on the bus . . . some kids who get on the bus are already stoned out of their gourds. . . . The most common place to buy

drugs is in the bathroom at school. . . . Actually I am pretty lucky . . . two of my girlfriends are dealers. Almost everybody is into pot or alcohol. If you don't smoke grass, there really isn't anything else to do at a party . . . you would just be sitting around while everybody else gets high. . . . There is a lot of peer pressure to participate. . . . Teachers are really stupid . . . in my one o'clock class the teacher is always talking about how nice the class is . . . it should be!! Half of the class is high on grass!

We asked these students the extent of drug usage in their school. They replied, "At least sixty or seventy percent of the kids smoke pot or take something like valium . . . but almost everybody has tried something, even if they don't use the stuff regularly."

Teachers must recognize that drugs are rapidly becoming a "way of life" for many students in the middle and high school. Elementary school teachers must be alerted to the fact that pot smoking, drinking and glue sniffing are occurring more and more in the early grades. Children as young as nine and ten years of age are beginning to experiment with drugs.

Rep. Lester Wolff (D., N.Y.), chairman of the Select Committee on Narcotics Abuse and Control, states: "The United States is the most pervasive drug-abusing nation in history." To support this statement, the Wolff committee provides the following statistics:

— Between 4 and 5 million kids between the ages of 11 to 17 are smoking pot on a reasonably regular basis.
— Since 1975, pot smoking has doubled in use by young people.
— 11% of *all* high school students (1 student in 9) are smoking pot on a *daily* basis. High school users smoke about 3½ joints per day.
— Pot smoking is now common among middle school students. Pot smoking is on the increase among 8 to 12 year olds.
— Of the 51% of the kids who smoked pot in high school in their senior year, 44% reported being high four to six hours per day.

81

The National Institute on Drug Abuse (NIDA) furnishes the following statistics:

— Before they graduate from high school about 80% of all kids will have smoked marijuana.
— 70% of the high school kids who smoke pot, admit to driving while they are "high" on marijuana. 75% of the high school children who drink alcohol, admit to driving while mildly intoxicated.
— 36% of all high school students surveyed stated they had smoked marijuana within the past thirty days.
— 68% of all persons between the ages of 18 to 25 have used pot.
— 20% of the children surveyed had tried tobacco or glue sniffing before the age of ten.
— 11% of all high school students have used cocaine.
— 14% of high school students surveyed had used PCP (angel dust).
— There are 4,000,000 problem drinkers in the 16-25 year old group. The average age of beginning to use alcohol is 12 years; some students report starting as early as 8-10 years.
— By the time they graduate from high school, nearly 75% of all students will have used alcohol.
— 40,000 teenagers are injured every year in auto accidents related to alcohol. 8,000 are killed in alcohol related accidents.

A Gallup Poll (1977) reported that only four percent (4%) of the American population used marijuana in 1969. By 1973, maijuana use had climbed to 12%. By 1977, there had been a 100% increase with 24% of the American population reporting that they used marijuana.

An NIDA report shows that alcohol and drug abuse is the third leading cause of illness in the United States. Reports also indicate that nearly 40% of emergency admissions to hospitals are related to substance abuse.

The Wolff committee reported that a study in California found that children usually begin to experiment with drugs in the fifth grade and some children reported using drugs as early as the second and third grade.

Dr. Robert DuPont, former director of NIDA summarizes the high incidence and problems of drug abuse in American school children. He states: "In all of history no young people have ever used drugs regularly on a mass scale. Therefore, our youngsters are, in effect, making themselves guinea pigs in a tragic national experiment. Thus far, our research clearly suggests that we will see horrendous results."

Types of Abused Drugs

There are several ways in which one can group the most commonly abused drugs. For our purposes we will divide the drugs into four major groupings. These are: Depressants, Stimulants, Psychedelics and Psychotropics.

The *depressants* include narcotics, barbiturates, alcohol and inhalants. The *stimulants* include substances like caffeine, nicotine and cocaine. The *psychedelics* include cannabis (marijuana) and hallucinogens like LSD and PCP (angel dust). The *psychotropics* include the strong tranquilizers and anti-depressants like elavil.

Figure 5.1 is adapted from a chart published by the Drug Enforcement Administration, a division of the Department of Justice and provides helpful information on common types of drugs, the type of physical and psychological dependence and the symptoms under normal and excessive use. A more detailed chart is available from the Drug Enforcement Administration — the title of the chart is "Controlled Substances: Uses and Effects."

	Drug Type	Examples	Psychological Dependence
DEPRESSANTS	Barbiturates	Phenobarbital Nembutal Seconal	High
	Alcohol	Beer, wine	High
	Mild Tranquilizers	Librium, Valium, Miltown	Moderate
	Methaqualone	Quaalude	High
	Inhalants	Aerosols, Butyl Nitrite (Rush), Gas	High
	Narcotics	Opium Codeine Heroin Demoral	High High High High
PSYCHEDELICS	Cannabis	Hashish, Hash Oil, Marijuana	Moderate
	Hallucinogens	LSD PCP Mescaline	Low Low Low
STIMULANTS	Cocaine Caffeine Nicotine	Cocaine Coffee, coke Cigarettes, cigars	High Low High
PSYCHOTROPICS	Anti-depressants	Elavil	None
	Strong tranquilizers	Compazine, Thorazine	None

FIGURE 5.1 — CONTROLLED SUBSTANCE

Physical Dependence	Effects with Average Use	Effects with Excessive Use
High	Relaxed, euphoria, drowsiness, poor coordination, slurred speech, sleep	Brain and/or liver damage, confusion, sickness, withdrawal, death
Moderate		
Moderate		
High		
None	Relaxed, euphoria, poor coordination	Hallucinations, liver, kidney, bone marrow & brain damage, death
High Moderate High High	Constricted pupils, relaxed, relief of pain, drowsiness, euphoria	Lethargy, weight loss, impotence, convulsions, withdrawal pains, sickness, death
None	Dilated pupils, Relaxed inhibitions, lethargy, disoriented behavior, red eyes	Liver, lung damage, brain damage, memory loss, insomnia, possible psychosis
None None None	Illusions and hallucinations, poor depth perception	Prolonged delusions, panic, psychosis, death.
None None None	Increased blood pressure, insomnia, loss of appetite, restlessness	Restlessness, irritability; with nicotine: heart and lung damage, cancer. With cocaine: damage to nasal septum.
None	Initially: relaxed, drowsiness	Weakness, tremors, death.
None		

USES AND EFFECTS

85

Why Children Use Drugs

Peer pressure

Research shows that the greatest single cause for the use of drugs is pressure from the peer group. Probably the first big "test" in life — outside the realm of the family — is the pressure which is exerted by youngsters who are the same age or just slightly older.

Even in the first grade the child is influenced by his peer group. While the impact is relatively small, it does have an affect on the child's attitudes and opinions. In the first grade, the child may learn "group words," "toilet language" and silly poems like, "No more classes, no more books, no more teacher's dirty looks." Peers do teach children to model after the rest of the group.

In the early grades, however, the peer group's influence is relatively mild. The child will turn to the teacher and the parent for guidance and receive "superego" strength from these adults. He will value and abide by adult counsel. Most children will say to their playmates, "I cannot do that because my mother would not like it." Or, "The teacher said that we should walk in line and not talk with our neighbor." In the early school years, the child views adults as heroes and "best friends." These adults represent ideals the child would like to emulate.

About 11 or 12 years of age — and during the adolescent years, the desire to be liked and accepted by the peer group becomes of paramount importance and during this time the relative influence of the teacher and parent declines. Discipline techniques which were effective in the first, second and third grade will often "backfire." (Can you imagine a high school teacher saying, "I would like to see all my good citizens sit up straight and not talk to their neighbor!") In fact, some students will purposely go counter to the wishes of the teacher just to attain status in the peer group. Thus, if the teacher chastises a child — the youngster's status in the peer group may be increased.

Peer pressure in the pre-adolescent and adolescent years can often be more exacting and more cruel than at any

86

other time in life. The peer group can make a child's life seem almost unbearable and the desire to be liked by the peer group can be overwhelming at times.

Adolescent is a time of social-biological-psychological change. The child is undergoing tremendous physical changes within his body. In addition he is going from the world of childhood to the world of adulthood. Values are examined and questioned and the youngster begins to experiment with new ideas and new materials. In to-day's world, this experimentation can include driving an automobile at reckless speeds, testing authority in many areas, and taking drugs.

The earlier section on drug incidence showed that in many schools over 80% of all high school seniors have tried marijuana, tranquilizers, alcohol or other drugs. Some schools report the percentage is as high as 90-95%. In other words more high school seniors have experimented with drugs than youngsters who have not.

In our conversations with high school students they report that smoking grass or getting drunk is the "thing to do." Youngsters who have not tried drugs encounter tremendous peer pressure. One girl told us, "When I was in high school I did not have any friends who were not using grass. I seldom went to parties because there was so much pressure to get high. It is almost impossible to have friends if you don't use drugs."

Other reasons for using drugs

In addition to peer pressure, we should recognize that there are other factors which may be involved in causing children to use drugs.

One major factor in drug use among young people is that they view drugs as relatively harmless. There are several reasons for having this point of view. Children see their parents using tobacco and alcohol. They see their grandmother take valium. Our society has viewed drugs as part of our normal life-style. In addition, in the 60s, reports stated that marijuana was "less harmful than cigarettes." LSD was supposed to give you amazing insights into yourself. PCP was supposed to give the user a pleasant "high" and reveal a lovely world. Early medical research and government reports during that period were often vague and confusing. To-day the data on drug abuse is much clearer. Unfortunately, many teachers are unaware of the latest finding and continue to view drugs as relatively harmless. This lack of knowledge is particularly true in terms of marijuana use. (The reader should study the effects of continued drug use as.outlined in Figure 5.1. In addition, the reader is referred to the special drug bibliography at the end of this chapter.)

One reason that drugs are viewed as harmless rests with the mass media. In many TV shows the Super-heroes and MCs treat pot and other drugs in a casual manner. It is not unusual to hear hosts on shows like "Real People" and "The Johnny Carson Show" make light references to pot and other drugs . . . this give the appearance of acceptability. Some comedians use jokes with double meanings — one for the "straights," another for the drug users.

Popular music has many references to drugs, pot, getting drunk and getting high. For example one popular song tells of snorting cocaine and in an old Beatles songs, "Lucy in the Sky with Diamonds," the capitals refer to LSD.

Many books and magazines glamorize the drug culture. They promise that drugs will provide great new insights —enhance lives, encourage creativity and understanding. Magazines like "High Times," with a reader circulation of nearly 5 million, push the joys of drugs and drug use. Their motto is: "(This magazine) . . . is about your favorite leisure activities — pot, hash, coke, LSD and a host of other natural highs." Stores which sell drug paraphernalia (called "Head Shops") are open to children of all ages. Corner mini-markets with their cigarette papers, incense and clay pipes — all suggest to the youngster that using drugs is okay.

Another reason for increased drug use is accessibility. Grass and pills are readily available in most middle and high schools in American to-day. Children we have interviewed state that the best place to obtain drugs is at school.

Drugs create a feeling of excitement and doing something "naughty." They give some children the sense of doing something dangerous — like the old days when teenagers played "chicken." Even though youngsters may believe that some drugs are potentially dangerous, adolescents have a feeling that they will "live forever." They have a real sense that, "I cannot be killed . . . that happens to someone else . . . other guys have 'bad trips' . . . it won't happen to me."

There is a very distrubing reason for drug use in the case of pre-teens. In many situations children 8-10 years of age are first introduced to drugs by an older brother or sister. There is a high correlation between early use by a child who has a sibling already on drugs.

We should mention one other major reason why children use drugs. Drugs provide the user with a variety of feelings — some drugs can make you feel drowsy; others can help you to be more alert . . . you may feel like you are "taking off" or "floating" or like a blast of air is hitting you in the face. Drugs can make you happy, sad, help you remember, help you forget, help you feel accepted, more social, avoid a painful experience. Drugs can give you a feeling of self-assurance, daring and bravado.

Initially, many drugs *do* make you feel good. They give one a feeling of euphoria . . . they make you "temporarily" forget your troubles . . . your problems seem less or they seem to disappear altogether. When a person is "high" on drugs or alcohol, they usually feel happy and believe that they are in complete control.

It is easy to see how drugs have taken hold in our culture. They have become as common as mom and apple pie. If we are to help children face the drug issue we must understand their reasons for taking drugs. While the influence of the peer group is extremely strong, it does not mean that the adult world is powerless in its battle against drug use. Later in this chapter we will discuss some things the teacher can do to cope with the situation.

Signs of Drug Use By Your Students

Usually the first, and most common, drug used by children is marijuana. Marijuana is referred to as the "gateway drug" since, in most cases, persons who use other drugs have started their drug career by smoking pot. In addition to marijuana, some children under twelve begin by sniffing glue or using inhalants such as: aerosols, gasoline, correction fluid, paint thinner, cleaning agents and butyl nitrite. (See Figure 5.1 for effects of drug use.)

While it is not always possible to determine if children are using drugs, there are certain clues and symptoms which should alert the teacher to possible drug use.

— Listen to conversation. Be particularly alert to the conversation of your children. Quite often they will use drug terminology because it makes them feel "cool" or a more integral part of the drug culture. For example, if you hear one child ask another, "Can you do me a favor?" —the child may be asking for a joint. This does not mean that if you hear a child say "pot," he is a user. However, the teacher should check further into the child's activities. (See Appendix E for a glossary of drug terms.)

— Examine notebooks. Often "drug phrases" are written on the covers of notebooks and in texts, scrapbooks and yearbooks. Statements are often written like, "Power through Pot," "Let's mow the grass," "Fruit salad isn't just for fruits."

— Look for cigarette papers. We mentioned earlier that many adults feel that marijuana and other drugs are "harmless." Notice how many "nice" mom and pop stores and mini-markets sell cigarette papers. This is particularly true in neighborhood stores near schools and in the service stations which have "game rooms."

— Look for plastic or cellophane "baggies." These are used to hold marijuana. Look for other drug paraphernalia — pipes or containers to hide pot. One popular item in "head shops" is a harmless looking Coca-Cola can which has a false bottom. There is a frisbee available which will hide grass and has a "built-in" pipe for smoking pot.

— Look for magazines like "High Times" which are definitely pro-drug.

— Look for red eyes. Sometimes children come to school stoned or get high while in school. Favorite spots for smoking a joint are in a remote area of the schoolground or in the restroom. Youngsters may use eyedrops to remove the redness. One junior high student told us: "At parties we stop smoking grass about ten o'clock and then everybody starts putting Visine in their eyes." Look for "glassy eyes," dialated pupils, a fuzzy look. The child may have the appearance of looking "in the distance."

— Look for a sweet smell in the restrooms or on children's clothing.

— A chronic cough or chest pains. This symptom is usually not present in beginning pot smokers, but appears after continued use.

— More compliant. When people are high, they are usually more agreeable and compliant. Police often report that at rock concerts they encounter few fights. Marijuana tends to make the individual quite docile. Teachers should be alerted to youngsters who sit quietly (and seem removed from the situation) and smile weakly when spoken to.

— Fatigue and slurry speech. A funny or false laugh.

— A change in behavior. More moody, less attention to appearance, less productive, less concern about home or a change in attitude about school. Lowering of grades, not working home assignments, lessened interest in school related activities.

— More secretive. The youngster may give the appearance

of hiding objects and seems very secretive. One sometimes sees feelings of paranoia in persons who are using drugs.

— Little sense of time. A child who is stoned often has a distorted feeling of time. Events seem to be "speeded up." Ask a child to indicate the passage of one minute of time. A child who is high will usually think that a minute has passed after an interval of only 15 or 20 seconds.

Finally, it should be emphasized that many of these symptoms can indicate problems other than use of drugs. A child who continually stays up late to watch television will show signs of fatigue. There are many reasons why a child could get moody or begin to lose interest in school. The onset of the teen years can often create changes in behavior. However, in most children the onset of adolescence will be accompanied with heightened interest in several areas: more interest in the opposite sex, more attention to grooming and general appearance, increased interest in school functions and a new zest for life.

It is incumbent upon the teacher to be alert to all the signs mentioned above and to begin to ascertain the reasons which may be causing changes in behavior. Our experience has been that often children may be engaging in drug use . . . but home and school either neglect or refuse to observe the obvious signs that drug usage is taking place.

What Teachers Can Do To Curb Drug Abuse

In spite of the major problems associated with drug abuse, teachers and parents *can* stem the tide and reverse the process. This section contains specific suggestions which have been useful in helping children cope with the drug problem. In addition the special bibliography at the end of this chapter contains references which describe specific programs where parents and the schools have cooperated and been successful in attacking the drug problem. The concerned reader is encouraged to study the references and to contact the organizations listed in the bibliography.

The best time to stop drug abuse is to approach the problem before it actually becomes one. The old adage, an ounce of prevention is worth a pound of cure, is especially true in terms of drug abuse. We firmly believe that there will continue to be more outside pressures exerted on children to experiment with drugs at younger ages. Here are some suggestions which may be helpful:

1) Teachers and the administration need to compare notes in order to determine the extent of the problem in the school. In a number of situations we have found that the administration tries to pretend that there is no drug problem . . . somehow hoping that, if unnoticed, the problem will go away. We suggest that you consult resource people in the community who may be more familiar with the drug problem and can make concrete suggestions for dealing with drug abuse. Talk with social workers, psychologists, persons in family and children's services, police officials and persons from the court system.

2) Teachers need to learn more about drugs and their consequences. The purpose of this chapter is to make the teacher cognizant of the seriousness of the drug problem and how to deal with it. As teachers we need to be aware of the dire consequences of drug use. It is difficult to give counsel to students when they know more about drugs than we do. Students often have only "partial knowledge." For example, most students will insist that pot is "less dangerous than cigarettes." Unless the teacher is well informed, she cannot respond meaningfully to the student.

3) Help children learn more about drugs and their consequences. Children need to be more knowledgeable about drugs and drug abuse. Three references which are particularly helpful to use with children are: Janeczek, C. *Marijuana: Time for a closer look,* Mann, P. *Marijuana update,* and Mann, P. *Twelve is too old.*

Youngsters should be made aware of the consequences of taking drugs. There is a large body of research data available which conclusively shows that severe physical and psychological damage can result. Recent studies on marijuana, for example, show that continued use can cause memory loss, brain and liver damage as well as effect cellular metabolism and reproduction.

We must recognize that children need accurate information about the problems of growing up in today's world . . . who is really behind the drug traffic . . . why? What about crime . . . and its relation to drugs. We are not suggesting that you "scare kids to death," but to be more realistic about the problems in the world today.

4) Give children an accurate picture about their own physical and psychological development. Help children to understand the biological-social-psychological changes which are occurring as they approach adolescence. These changes often make growing up difficult but they lay the foundation for future adult development.

Children need to recognize that the pre-adolescent and adolescent years represent a time when the child learns how to deal with adversity and change. Problems with parents, school, work and the opposite sex are all normal parts of growing up. One of the major developmental tasks of the teen years is to learn to cope with stress and learn problem solving skills. However, drugs interfere with this decision making process. Drugs cloud the issue . . . they cause the child to delay decisions and avoid reality. When he is "high," his problems seem to disappear and the youngster begins to feel that drugs have "solved" his problems. Unfortunately this type of attitude inhibits an extremely important phase of growth and development.

5) Hold discussions with children about drugs, drug use and peer group pressure. In too many instances, adults are prone to "preach" to children about the drugs. Have discussions and allow the children to voice their concerns. In our research for this chapter, we have learned that most youngsters will openly talk about drugs and their role in teen culture. The teacher can provide some guidance by suggesting specific areas for discussion such as, "The role of the peer group in drugs" or "The problems of saying

'No' when offered a drink or a joint" or "Alternatives to drugs."

Psychologists often use the term, "Concerned Listening" or "Active Listening." These terms mean that the teacher not only hears what the child is *saying,* but what the child is *feeling.* It means that the person listens to the comment, rather than thinking about their own response. It means that the listener — listens — rather than giving a quick or easy response.

Coupled with the concept of "Concerned Listening" is "Empathic Responding." This means that *after listening* — the teacher gives the person a response which shows that she understands how the individual feels and what the individual is saying. *All too often teachers are not good listeners. As the child is talking, they begin to frame their own reply, rather than listening to the comment (and the spirit of the comment).* When teachers do not listen and do not show a real concern or empathy, they merely turn children away from them. They are, in effect, showing children that they really do not care.

In addition to the concepts of "Active Listening" and "Empathic Responding" there are two other techniques which can be helpful in communicating with others.

We have found one technique that is quite helpful in holding discussions and is particularly useful in teaching students how to hold a discussion. This method of discussion is called "Circular Response." The participants make a circle. The first person in the circle begins by talking about the subject. They may make any comment they wish. (In some instances, there may be a time limit on each discussant's contribution.) After the first person talks, the person seated to that person's right has his turn. The discussion proceeds around the circle and each person must contribute.

The circular response technique does have two rules: First, the contributor *cannot verbally disagree* with any of the preceding statements. Second, if the individual does not have any new ideas, he must summarize the comments of the last contributor. (The idea behind these rules is simple. If the person *knows in advance* that he cannot disagree — or get into an argument — he will listen since he must either *add* to the discussion or *summarize* the previous contributor's comments.) Notice that this discussion technique is similar to empathic responding. It forces the participants to listen to the contributor rather than "cutting him off."

Another technique in effectively communicating with others is the concept of the "You Statement" and the "I Message." The "You Statement" has the effect of placing blame and creating guilt. The "I Message" has the effect of presenting a person with your own honest feelings and suggesting possible alternatives to the problem.

Examples: *In the "You Statement" the teacher might say:*

"You are talking. Do you always have to run your mouth?"

With the "I Message" the teacher could state:

"I cannot teach the class when you are talking, it is very difficult for the other children to hear."

Instead of: "You are a slow poke! Must you always be the last one to finish?"

Try: "I notice that you are having difficulty in getting finished. I wonder if we could find some ways to help you get your work done more quickly?"

Notice that the "You Statement" has the effect of criticism or incrimination. It sounds like an assault on the other person. In addition, the "You Statement" creates a negative emotional climate. It immediately places the child on the defensive — and often makes them *reply* with a "You Statement" of their own! The "I Message," on the other hand, is given in a calm but firm manner. It shows the individual the problem with clarity and may provide the person some suggestions on ways behavior can be improved or altered.

Another helpful communication technique is the concept of "I win, you win." All too often we place people in an "I win, you lose" situation. This action usually places the individual on the defensive and he responds, "No you don't win, in fact . . . I am going to win and you are going to lose!" Unfortunately in many "I win, you lose" situations, both parties may lose. The teacher should try to create situations in which both parties can win — and keep their respect.

6) The importance of openness and acceptance. Children must realize that your approach to them is open and above-board. They must feel that they can trust you and that you are accepting of their ideas. For many children, their teacher is the "Court of last resort." They realize that their parents and others will not accept them or their behavior . . . and the teacher may represent the only member of the adult world to whom they can turn for reassurance, counsel and advice.

7) Enlist the aid of parents. Many parents recognize the seriousness of the drug problem. Most of these parents are ready and willing to work in cooperation with the school to meet the drug problem "head on." We find that often parents are already *individually concerned* but do not know where to turn or what to do. When a parent finds their child is on drugs, there may be a tendency to withdraw from other parents. They may feel guilt and believe that the problem is entirely their fault.

One of the most effective solutions to the drug epidemic has been parents' groups. In most cases where parents have organized, compared notes, and attacked the problem in force, drug use has decreased. If your school does not yet have a drug problem, we suggest that you work with parents in establishing an information program to make parents knowledgeable about drugs and to alert them to the facts concerning drug abuse. (The reader is referred to the special bibliography at the end of this chapter which lists specific references concerning the organization of parent groups.)

8) Getting outside help. If there are already a lot of drugs in your school you do, indeed, have a big problem. As stated earlier in this section — the best time to stop drug abuse is to approach the problem before it becomes one.

However, if the problem already exists, the teacher needs supplemental aid and assistance. Since the teacher is not adequately trained to handle this type situation, she needs to enlist the help of the administration, the parents and other outside agencies. We have found that when a child is deeply involved in drugs (and may be a poly-drug user — or into hard drugs) a referral is absolutely necessary. We should point out that some parents may resent your suggestion that they need outside help. As mentioned earlier, the parent may feel guilty or even deny that a problem exists. In these cases we suggest that the teacher consult with the school social worker or school psychologist as well as her principal on ways to approach the parent and the best way to make a referral. In some instances the principal or the school psychologist will be the most appropriate person to deal directly with the parent. If your shool does not have professional support personnel, we suggest contacting city or county family and children's services (or other appropriate agencies) for assistance in ways to handle this problem.

Special Resource Bibliography on Drugs

Books & Pamphlets

The books and pamphlets below will give the teacher a good beginning library. Materials which are (*) are particularly valuable.

*Barbour, J. *Marijuana and your child.* New York: The Associated Press, 1981.

*Fornaciari, S. *How to talk to kids about drugs.* Bethesda, MD: Potomac Press (Division of Pacific Institutes for Research), 1979.

Hart, R. *Bitter grass.* Kansas City, MO: Psychoneurologia Press, 1980.

*Janeczek, C. *Marijuana: Time for a closer look.* Columbus, OH: Healthstar Publications, 1980.

*Mann, Peggy. *"Marijuana update,"in Reader's Digest* in December 1979 and May 1980. (Note: These two articles appear in a special *Reader's Digest* reprint.)

*Mann, Peggy. *Twelve is too old.* New York: Doubleday, 1980. (Note: This book is a novel for pre-adolescents which realistically deals with marijuana.)

*NIDA. *Drug abuse prevention for your family.* Washington, DC: DHEW Publication #79-584. (One of a series of seven pamphlets on drugs published by NIDA.)

*NIDA. *Parents, Peers and Pot.* Washington, DC: DHHS Publication #80-812. 1979.

Nahas, G., & Frick, H. *Drug abuse in the modern world.* New York: Pergamon Press, 1981.

Nahas, G. *Keep off the grass.* New York: Pergamon Press, 1979.

*Rusche, Sue. *How to form a families in action group in your community.* Atlanta: DeKalb Families in Action, Inc. (mailing address: Box 15053, Atlanta, GA 30333), 1979.

U. S. Department of Justice. *Project DAWN: Annual report, 1979.* Washington: Supt. of Documents, 1980.

Organizations to Contact for Further Information and Material.

American Council on Marijuana and Other Psychoactive Drugs. 521 Park Avenue, New York, NY 10021.

Citizens for Informed Choices on Marijuana (CICOM). 300 Broad Street, Stamford, CT 06901.

Families in Action, Inc. Box 15053, Atlanta, GA 30333.

National Institute of Drug Abuse (NIDA). 5600 Fishers Lane, Rockville, MD 20857.

Parent Resource Institute for Drug Education (PRIDE). University Plaza, Georgia State University, Atlanta, GA 30303.

National Federation of Parents for Drug Free Youth. Box 57217, Washington, DC 20037.

Learning Objectives For Chapter Five:

After reading Chapter Five, "Drugs: A special problem," the reader should be able to:

1. Have an overview of the drug problem in the United States.
2. Have knowledge of the incidence of drugs, especially as they impact on young children.
3. Name the four major drug categories: Depressants, stimulants, psychedelics and psychotropics. In addition the student should be able to list some of the common drugs and symptoms of excessive use.
4. Discuss the role of the peer group in terms of drug use.
5. In addition to peer group pressure, list other reasons which may lead to involvement in drugs.

6. Recognize "signs" or symptoms which may indicate drug use by youngsters.
7. Discuss several things teachers can do to help curb drug abuse. (The text lists eight things the teacher might consider. The reader should be able to discuss each suggestion and show how these could be implemented.)
8. Recognize the importance of discussing drugs and drug abuse. The student should be able to define the following terms and show how these concepts relate to group and/or individual discussions.

   a. Concerned Listening; Active Listening
   b. Empathic Responding
   c. Circular Response
   d. "You Statements" and "I Messages"
   e. "I win, you win"

Chapter Six

Classroom Management
And The Exceptional Child

Virginia A. Boyle, Ph.D.

Within the school setting, exceptional children are classified as those children who have some physical, intellectual or emotional handicap which interferes with, or depresses learning and adaptation to school. The handicaps are seldom directly responsible for deviations in adaptive behavior in the sense that they cause the student to be aggressive, obstinate, uncooperative, withdrawn or overly active. However, attentional deficits, high or low activity levels, or emotional reactions and actions associated with the handicapping condition can directly affect the behavior of the student and the type of response he gives in the classroom.

It is important to recognize that exceptional children with any single or multiple type of handicapping condition are more like "normal" students than they are different. They are the same because learning is important to them, making friends is important to them, relating to the teacher is important to them, playing and having fun is important to them, feeling worthwhile is important to them, and feeling that they have a contribution to make and something to give — is important to them. They have essentially the same feelings as other students in that they have happy, glad, sad, mad, frustrated, scared and anxious feelings. They react to situations most of the time with the same feelings — if they have difficulty learning, they become frustrated and feel bad about themselves; if they have successes they feel good about themselves. Just as with any student, they are hurt when someone is critical of their behavior or rejects them.

They are different from other students in several ways. For example, they may require: (1) some adaptation in the physical setting to accommodate their physical handicap, (2) some adaptation in material and informational presentation, (3) a specialized structure to help in prompting more appropriate (and efficient) behavioral responses to various settings. In addition, the teacher must be aware of the limitations associated with a specific handicap. In this manner the teacher can be more realistic about the quality and quantity of response she can expect.

Major causes of handicaps

It is important to understand that handicaps may be caused by a variety of agents or events. These can be categorized into basically four divisions: physical or biological, cultural, family rearing and educational.

Physical or biological causes have a wide range including: (1) some type of genetically related or congential aberration such as Downs Syndrome or microcephaly which causes mental retardation, (2) a traumatic event which is directly insulting to the neurological system as in encephalitis associated with red measles, (3) a fall on the head which may lead to specific learning disabilities, mental retardation, deafness or blindness.

While the cultural milieu is not usually considered the precursor to a handicapping condition, it certainly can be one. When a student comes from a different culture he may have to contend with language differences as well as varying expectations with regard to behavior.

103

Family rearing practices constitute a significant force in terms of the child's attitudes and behaviors. The family "sets the stage" by teaching the child coping styles which are used in dealing with an array of emotions and emotionally arousing situations. There is little doubt that the influence of the family has a major impact on the development of the child.

Education can be a causative agent of student handicaps. Research shows that the early years of education can predispose a student to like or dislike school, to feel motivated or not motivated to perform well in school, to feel trust that those important adults in the classroom will guide him in learning important basic skills. Moreover, should a teacher be poorly prepared to teach certain skills, the student may accumulate gaps in his educational experience. These gaps will handicap him in the mastery of other skills and knowledge. The mobility of the population can play a role in producing educational gaps because the student who moves about frequently may miss opportunities to learn certain skills.

Understanding the causes of handicaps and the associated behavioral management difficulties is beneficial in that methods of treatment sometimes can be aimed directly at the cause. For example, if neurological difficulties are responsible for an overly high activity level, and the student has a short attention span, a physician may perscribe medication which can increase the student's ability to attend to relevant information. Family practices and attitudes can be altered to bring about changes in the student's behavior. However, there are times that the casual agent is unclear, or unknown, or there is no known manner in which the cause can be affected. In these instances the teacher must deal directly with the behavior and utilize methods that modify or change the behavior.

In the process of deciding how student behavior is to be managed or changed, teachers tend to focus on the student as the object of change. *In fact, the first person who must change in the process of changing behavior is the teacher.* The teacher must change in her attitudes, expectations, goals, and responses to the student. In this process the *last*

104

person to change is the student and only in response to those changes made by the teacher.

In guiding the behavior of the exceptional student, most management techniques — such as those listed by the authors — are equally effective with exceptional students. At times, however, some aspect of the student's handicapping condition may prevent the teacher from utilizing certain techniques or render these "usual" techniques less effective. When this occurs it is essential that the teacher reassess her approaches, expectations and setting.

Because exceptional children are typically more like "normal" than they are different, most "normal" management principles apply, but often must be emphasized more strongly than with normal children. Consequently, key principles will be listed below which, in many instances, are a repetition of ideas presented in other chapters of this book. However, they bear repetition and reiteration because of their importance in the management of exceptional children.

Key Principles In Working With Exceptional Children

Rapport or "Honey catches more flies than vinegar"
The necessity of establishing rapport with exceptional students bears much emphasis. It is an idea that teachers tend to forget particularly in times of frustration and stress. Exceptional students are people and, like most people, they tend to be more cooperative with persons with whom they have established a positive relationship. Students wish to please those people whom they feel believe in them, have confidence in them and like them. Disapproval, correction and criticism from people they like, and by whom they feel liked, is more potent and more important to the student to avoid. Rapport is the power, the drive behind techniques of management that the teacher uses. Without positive rapport, management techniques are much less effective and some are not effective at all.

Modeling or "Monkey-see, Monkey-do"

In chapter three the authors have emphasized the importance of modeling as a major mode of learning. Students tend to mimic and imitate those behaviors they see other people use, particularly if those behaviors are effective in obtaining those things that the observing student finds desirable. Students are also inclined to imitate teacher behaviors and may adopt some behaviors as their own. This idea is particularly important when we consider that students learn how to cope with many feelings and problems through observing or even reading of how others cope. Values, attitudes, morals, ethics and emotional controls are learned from others.

Consistency or "Just one more time"

Many teachers tend to believe that once a specific behavior has been punished or reinforced — that behavior should be eliminated or "permanentized" forever. However, this is not the case. In order to establish or alter a behavior pattern, one must consistently "water and fertilize" the grouping of desired behaviors. The newer the behavior or the older the behavior, the more consistent the behavior modifier must be. For example, suppose the teacher wants a child to hold up his hand before speaking in a class discussion. It will be necessary for the teacher to prompt, redirect and reward that behavior daily until it becomes apparent that the behavior is well established. For some students, the behavior might become well established within two weeks, while other students may need on-going usage of these techniques over several years. This is particularly true of impulsive, hyperactive students who have to expend a great deal of time and effort in controlling impulses.

Punishment and redirection or "Stop-Go"

In behavior management, teachers tend to focus on undesirable conduct. While it is important for the teacher

106

to identify behaviors which are innapropriate and which interfere with learning, it is even more important for them to identify acceptable conduct. When the student stops acting in one way, he will replace the extinguished behavior with another. The wise teacher is one who identifies appropriate behavior outcomes. If the teacher does not do so, the student is apt to elect to act in ways which are equally inappropriate and ineffective. Once a behavior is stopped through various forms of punishment, the teacher should provide structure, prompt or redirect the student to appropriate behavior and follow that behavior with a pleasant consequence. Research shows that this combination of techniques is one of the more effective forms of behavioral change.

External factors that provide sources of control

There are many factors within a school and classroom setting that can be used as a source of external control for students. Some of the familiar sources of control consist of rules of behavior and enforcement of these rules, the classroom curriculum (when a child is learning academic material, it is difficult for him to "act out"), curricular schedule, classroom routines, the physical arrangement of a classroom, directions from the teachers concerning classroom assignments and selective placement of students who have control problems.

Teachers seldom think of many of these as sources of control, yet they know that if they have not planned their "learning day" in terms of student needs and interests, they can expect more behavior difficulties that day. Thus, a teacher who invests time in developing daily lesson plans will be amply rewarded, particularly by those students who have control problems. These plans should include considerations of: what students need to learn that day, the skills the students need in learning the material, the length of time that the student can likely attend to that material, the type of learning format which would facilitate learning, the amount of material the student can handle in terms of self direction and self control and the interests of the student.

While these factors are true of "normal" students, they are even more relevant for the exceptional student. Exceptional children may have severe limitations in the knowledge and skills they bring to the learning situation. The special child may need extra cues in the learning presentation, selected types of learning formats, as well as more frequent breaks in learning due to a short attention span and greater fatigue. Exceptional students may not be able to respond to some types of formats because they do not have the self motivation or self control to utilize them. In addition this student may need greater amounts of warmth and encouragement from the teacher in order to persevere when they feel so discouraged about their abilities.

Classroom control is, in the mind of many educators and lay persons, associated with the degree of punishment which a teacher or administrator has at her fingertips. While many different forms of punishment are certainly needed in the classroom, they should not be considered the major source of classroom control. For the exceptional student, who may have greater difficulty in establishing emotional and behavioral controls, this would mean more negativism — and an increased loss of self-respect. It could also result in negative attitudes toward learning, the school and the teacher. Control is most effectively established when it offers the student direction plus information on ways he can accomplish what is expected. Positive control speaks to those techniques used by the teacher which not only direct and instruct the student in what is expected, but those which offer support and encouragement to do so. This can be provided through the learning situations teachers establish, the types of structure utilized, plus the recognition and praise given the student when he is performing as expected. Students need rewards and confirmations for those things they do which are right more than they need punishments for things they do which are not desirable.

There are many other types of external controls which can be utilized by the classroom teacher. Some specific suggestions are outlined below:

1. Follow difficult, frustrating assignments with activities which are rewarding and which offer the student a means of energy and tension release. For example, providing each student with a sheath of old newspapers which they can tear vigorously on command for one minute (and clean up the mess afterwards); foot or potato sack races outside; the vigorous and lively singing of songs. To effectively use these activities, it must be made clear that the "acting out" student may have to be relieved of the opportunity to participate in the activity or the entire class may lose the opportunity. This includes waiting patiently for an activity to start on teacher command and stop promptly when terminated. It also includes responsibility for clean up.

2. Using students to recognize and praise other pupils when they are acting as expected and ignoring them when they are violating an expectation or rule.

3. Role playing can be used in activities where the expectations are explained to the students and role played. This is a particularly helpful activity to employ when expectations are complex and where students need to be conditioned to respond to teacher cues such as hand signals.

4. The teacher should be alerted to transitions. Remember that transitions offer the greatest reason and opportunity for misbehavior. This is particularly true for the exceptional child. Transitions should be well planned and expectations made clear. For example, if a class does not handle the transition to lunch as quietly and smoothly as needed, the teacher may need to review the entire procedure with her students. She may wish to introduce some type of structure which aids in a transition. ("The green table can go; the blue table is quiet, so it can go . . . etc.) The teacher may wish to have the children "role play" the transition and give recognition when students respond appropriately. In the next chapter, the subject of transitions is treated in greater detail.

5. Use "positive thinking" exercises with your students. Have the children sit quietly for a few minutes, heads on

arms, in a relaxed position — "just like a loose, limp Raggedy Ann doll." While in this mode, ask them to *really concentrate* on how they are going to do a certain task —how they are going to feel in doing the task, the effort they will expend, how satisfied they will feel when they have accomplished their goal. This technique is particularly effective with a new assignment or when a task may be difficult and frustrating.

From external control to internal control "Yours to Mine"

When students are misbehaving in the classroom, and interfering with learning and classroom procedures, it becomes necessary for the teacher to establish outside controls or structures which aid in reducing or eliminating inappropriate behaviors. Classroom rules are an example of such an external structure. In training students to improve their behavior it becomes important to develop a system whereby the rules and reinforcements begin to belong to the student, that is, they begin to become "internalized structures." In the final analysis, this is the "bottom line" — we want our students to be able to abide by the rules because they see the need to do so. In Chapter Seven, the concept of internal and external discipline will be explored in greater detail.

Student punishment may be punishing to the teacher

In selecting behaviors which must be stopped by punishment, it is important for the teacher to choose punishments that are easy to apply. If the action becomes painful for the teacher, she will be less apt to employ the technique and become inconsistent in treating the behavior. For example, the teacher may say, "Buddy, if you do that one more time I will have to send you to the principal or I will have to paddle you." If the teacher does not really want to send the student to the principal because it could make her look badly in his eyes or if she does not want to paddle the student because it is painful for her to act in this manner — she will be most reluctant to follow up on her threat. Buddy then learns that he can continue to misbehave with little fear of the consequences.

It is also important to realize that in most instances the punishment does not have to match the deed in terms of power or intensity. It is important, however, that the deed be punished — and punished consistently — if it is to be extinguished. Thus the key is selection of a punishment which is consistent with the teacher's philosophy and one which she can apply consistently with little or no hesitation. In the final analysis, it is not necessary for the teacher to be punished when the student is punished.

Be a good scout: Be prepared

Teachers seldom do a lot of behavior management planning prior to the arrival of new students. Usually they do not think through the acceptable or undersirable behaviors they may witness — nor the reinforcements which might be appropriately meted out. This type of preplanning is beneficial, however, since it will expedite student adaptation to the classroom. In teaching exceptional children it is particularly important because of the higher incidence of maladaptive behavior that is associated with this group. (See Figure 6.1)

Prior to opening day, the teacher should make a list of potential nonadaptive behaviors which she may expect from her students. It is also helpful to list comfortable punishments and redirections which she feels would be effective in teaching students the desired behaviors. Teachers tend to become emotional and overreact when they are presented with student behaviors which they did not expect and feel incapable of handling. As the teacher becomes more skilled in dealing with nonadaptative behaviors, she will be better equipped to handle them without becoming overly upset.

Figure 6.1
NEGATIVE BEHAVIORS ASSOCIATED WITH
EXCEPTIONAL CHILDREN

Exceptionality	*Key Characteristics*
Learning Disabled (L.D.)	Hyper or hypo activity, negative attitudes, testing behavior
Mental Retardation (M.R.) (Mild)	Passivity, non-initiating, testing of limits, limited social skills
Emotionally Disturbed	Wide variety of symptoms. May display every characteristic of L.D. Extremely fearful, crying, selective mutism, explosive episodes, "acting" out, tantrums
Visually Impaired	Overly dependent, extremely shy, fearful, withdrawn, explosive episodes, self stimulating behavior, tactile behavior, mobilization problems
Hearing Impaired	Loud, acting out, socially limited, communication difficulties, withdrawn
Neurologically Impaired	Language delay, loud abrasive, limit testing, erratic behavior, high activity level, explosive episodes, impulsivity, short attention span
Chronically Ill (Asthmatics, diabetics, etc.)	Quick fatigue, low energy level, psychosomatic complaints, overly dependent

The more regressed, the more structured

There are occasions when a teacher becomes heir to an immature class of students — or a situation where many members of the class are "late maturers." When this occasion arises, the teacher must recognize that these students have fewer internal controls and thus need greater external control and structure. The teacher needs to increase those structures and directions in the classroom which provide the immature student with firmer direction and redirection. The teacher may have to resort to employing a more rigid and traditional classroom arrangement. She will need a greater array of comfortable punishments and redirection. In addition, she will have to work constantly to discover the positives in those immature students in order to provide them with the positive reinforcement, rapport and encouragement which they need.

Power Struggles: The winner may be the loser

At some pont every teacher has some students who present themselves as belligerent, defiant and test the teacher's authority. There are some hyperactive children who give this appearance but who, in fact, are simply not aware of the boundaries or the rules. That is, they are not intentionally setting out to defy or overrun the authority.

There are other students, many times children with learning difficulties or emotional problems, who have established a pattern of defiance and limit testing. They may argue with the teacher over various issues, they may deliberately participate in an act of defiance or they may persist in trying to obtain special privileges.

These kinds of students are particularly difficult for teachers to handle because of the emotions they arouse in the teacher — usually as a result of their subtle or blatant disrespect for the teacher's authority. It is difficult for the teacher not to react by getting sucked into a power struggle with the student. The teacher may begin to argue back or begin to make strong assertions of her authority by being punitive. It is true that once into a power struggle, the teacher must win, but in winning she has also become a loser in that she will begin to lose her effectiveness with the student. In losing the battle, the student feels put down and may become angry toward the teacher.

Therefore, it is important for the teacher to begin to recognize those times when the gauntlet has been thrown out by the student. Perhaps the most helpful clue to the teacher in identifying the potential onset of a power struggle is by being aware of her reaction to the student. When the teacher feels threatened and frustrated by the student there is always a possibility that a struggle is "on the verge."

How does one respond to a ploy by the student which

would initiate a power struggle? The teacher can simply ignore the comments and acts of the student. She could verbalize what she thinks the student is doing — comment on what she thinks the outcome might be, and then indicate her desire not to become involved in a situation which would lead to those kind of results, and then ask the student what he really wants. Sometimes merely asking the student to verbalize the rule or the expectation will bring a halt to a power struggle. The issue then becomes —how many different approaches the teacher can develop to avoid the power struggle.

Supplementary Factors That Contribute To Student Control

Medication

Medication can prove useful in reducing the high activity level of a hyperactive student or the anxiety of an emotionally disturbed child. The use of medication in management of behavior has been over emphasized by educators and there has been a resulting backlash on the part of parents and physicians. It is not the professional responsibility of the teacher to determine whether a student would benefit from medication, that is the responsibility of the physician and parent. All the teacher can be responsible for in relation to medication is suggesting to a parent that they consider consulting their physician for examination and recommendation. A teacher is not professionally licensed to administer the medication, even though many do and are placing themselves in jeopardy by doing so. They can keep medication for students and make it available to them.

There are some hyperactive children who, on taking the proper type and dosage of medication, change dramatically in their behavior. There are others who can attend somewhat better and we may see some improvement in behavior. There are some children where the behavior has not improved and they may even be more active as a result of medication.

Cooperation of the home

Parents of exceptional children often feel guilty and responsible for their child's handicap. They can easily become defensive about problems which arise in school and become uncooperative with the school. At times they may attempt to blame the school for their child's difficulty or may attempt to avoid any discussions about the problems their child is presenting in the classroom. In their attempt to undo or deny their child's handicap, they may be overly protective and quite unrealistic about their expectations for their child and his teacher.

One of the biggest complaints parents of exceptional children have is that the only time they are contacted by the teacher or school is when their child is presenting problems. For some students who are having major adjustment difficulties, these calls may be quite frequent. If the teacher can stand back and look at what is being said, she may realize that in developing any type of working relationship, it is better to start off on a positive and not the negative.

If a teacher knows of a student who may present problems in the classroom, she should contact the parents and take the time and opportunity to visit with them before the child's problems are discussed at a future conference. Via notes and telephone contacts, the teacher should take the time to provide the parents with positive feedback on the areas where their child is doing well. (Refer to the bibliography. The chapter on troubled children by Gearheart and Weishahn has some excellent suggestions on parent communication.)

Throughout the school year the teacher should work to provide the parents with a balanced, but realistic picture of their child's progress. The teacher should be very open about the problems she sees with the child in his role as a student. The focus should be objective and should not cast blame on the parents or the teacher. It is perfectly acceptable, even desirable, for the teacher to identify problems the child presents with which the teacher is having difficulty. Often parents can make constructive suggestions to the teacher by sharing techniques which have worked well for them. The relationship between the teacher and the parents should be one in which both identify problems that need attention and on which they can work together to arrive at solutions.

Psychotherapy and counseling

There are times when a student can benefit from psychotherapy or counseling with a trained mental health professional. The parents and entire family may also need some professional help. A suggestion from the teacher can often prompt the parents to investigate whether this type of service is needed.

Once a child, parents or family are in psychotherapy or counseling, there may be important information which the teacher and mental health professional can share. Information can be shared between parties only when the parents give their consent. Needless to say, all information shared is highly confidential as is all information that a teacher normally has available on a child. This information should not be discussed with anyone who is not professionally involved with the child without the consent of the parents.

Special education services

Most exceptional students are eligible for various types of special educational services. Services can range from psychoeducational evaluation to consultation with the classroom teacher to placement, either partial or full-time in a special education class or program. Special education services are always a supplementary program to the regular classroom unless the student utilizes special education services more than half the day. This means the regular classroom teacher retains responsibility for the instruction the child receives. At times there may be disagreement between the regular teacher and special education personnel as to how a situation should be handled. Of course, it is best to work out some type of solution or compromise to avoid placing the student in a situation where he suffers from the conflict between the professionals. If this is not possible, it is wise to bring in administrative personnel — and if necessary the parents —to aid in resolving the conflict. The conflict should never be allowed to interfere with instruction and management techniques being provided to the student.

Tutors

There are times when a student can benefit from tutorial instruction outside of school. The parents may be unable to help their child with homework assignments or projects without undue pressure or frustration. Tutors can sometime aid in helping the child establish work-study skills which are unknown to the parents. As such, it is to a teacher's benefit to develop a list of tutors who are reputable, conscientious and work well with youngsters.

In summary

It is hoped that these suggestions, techniques and key principles will be helpful to the teacher as she works with the exceptional child. However, as we mentioned in the beginning of the chapter, *it is important to recognize that exceptional children with any single or multiple type of handicapping condition are more like "normal" students than they are different.*

Learning Objectives For Chapter Six:

After reading Chapter Six, "Classroom Management and the Exceptional Child," the reader should be able to:

1. Recognize that the exceptional child is more like the "normal" child than different.
2. Identify and list the four major causes of handicaps: Physical or biological, cultural, family rearing and educational.
3. Without the aid of references, list and discuss _____ key principles which are important in working with exceptional children. (The text described *ten* key principles; the reader can set her own criterion for adequate knowledge of this item.) These key principles include: the importance of rapport, modeling, consistency, punishment and redirection, internal and external factors, structure and struggles for power.
4. Discuss some of the negative behaviors that may be associated with exceptional children.
5. Discuss the teacher's role in terms of medication.
6. Discuss the importance of working closely with the home and family.

Chapter Seven

Techniques Of
Classroom Management

Perhaps the single most important factor in controlling classroom behavior is the teacher's ability in making the subject matter stimulating and enjoyable. When this is accomplished, children become involved and the teacher will experience few discipline or management problems. If the teacher presents her subject matter material in an interesting and relevant manner, the children will be attentive. If, on the other hand, the learning climate is dull; the discussions irrelevant; the material too advanced; the assignments inappropriate — students become bored and frustrated. The result? Children start to misbehave.

Our research has shown that sometimes the teacher becomes so busy and ego-involved, she is totally unaware of her behaviors. At times, she may unknowingly use rough techniques, she may avoid the aggressive child; ignore the passive individual and devote a disproportionate amount of time to the cute, verbal, attractive youngster. Teaching is a very difficult job — teachers have to juggle many factors and constantly change and adjust their priorities. In Appendix D, we have included some items which are designed to help the teacher assess herself by analyzing her teaching methods and determining if she is meeting her overall goals.

The earlier chapters of this treatise have been primarily directed at discipline in terms of the individual child. However, the principles and techniques which have been discussed are, for the most part, equally applicable to small groups or to an entire class. For example, consistency is important whether or not the teacher is disciplining a single individual or a total group. As mentioned in Chapter Four, rough control techniques are generally detrimental and actually have no greater effect in gaining compliance than do milder influence techniques. The principles of reinforcement theory are also appropriate in class settings and can aid the teacher in the utilization of group management techniques. In addition, there are some strategies which one should consider when working with an entire group. The purpose of this chapter is to examine these areas and their implications for the teacher.

Contagion Effects

In Chapter Four we discussed the ripple effect in discipline. We noted that the ripple effect is the influence a control technique exerts — not on the target child — but on the other children in the classroom as the IT "ripples out" from the target child. Chapter Four discussed several effects in this connection: When the IT was clear — and when the IT was firm, the audience children responded with increased conformance. On the other hand, when the teacher employed a technique which was very harsh or rough (e.g., being angry, highly punitive, shouting), the entire class became apprehensive, less involved in their work and showed general signs of anxiety and restlessness.

In other words there is a contagion factor in classroom management. Therefore the teacher must be aware that children can also learn the rules of behavior indirectly — as they observe the manner in which the teacher disciplines others in the classroom. The following examples may be helpful.

Ms. Harris is working with a reading table. At an adjacent table three boys are playing with a lotto game. One boy, apparently bored with the game, pushes his lotto cards on the floor and leaves the table. Ms. Harris looks up and says, "Clark, come back and pick up your mess." At this instant, Ms. Harris is distracted. Seeing that the teacher is not looking, Clark turns around and goes to the easel. Roscoe, a second boy at the lotto table says, "Ms. Harris, Clark didn't pick up his cards." Ms. Harris does not respond.

Roscoe shrugs his shoulders and scatters his cards on the floor. Marvin, the third boy at the table, laughs and begins tossing cards in the air saying, "It's raining lotto . . . it's raining lotto!"

Annemarie happens to be walking by the table. She picks up several cards from the floor, tosses them in the air and mimics Marvin, "It's raining lotto . . . it's raining lotto!" Roscoe picks up the lotto box and hits Annemarie over the head saying, "Get outta here . . . this is our game." At this moment Ms. Harris looks up from the reading table and says, "What is going on here?"

Ms. Days, a student teacher, is giving directions for a science experiment to the entire class. While the lesson is going on Gail and Ralph periodically whisper to each other. At one point Grace joins in the conversation. Evidently Ralph says something funny because Gail and Grace begin to snicker. Grace turns to Wilma (at the next table) and whispers something to her. Wilma looks at Ralph and starts to laugh. Ralph and Gail start to laugh out loud. Grace whispers something else to Wilma and both start laughing. Ms. Days stops her lesson and says, "Grace, I saw that!"

In the two examples presented both teachers were negligent in pursuing any definite course of action. As a result, deviant behavior began to spread. In the case of Ms. Harris, she failed to "follow up" on her original admonition to Clark. Upon seeing this, Roscoe duplicated Clark's behavior. Marvin likewise became contaiged and drew

Annemarie into the misbehavior which finally resulted in her being accosted by Roscoe.

Ms. Days, the student teacher, waited too long and allowed the misbehavior to spread. Starting with Gail and Ralph, it soon encompassed Grace. Shortly thereafter the misbehavior spread to Wilma at a nearby table. Wilma, in turn began to laugh and her laughter rippled back to infect the original twosome.

Let us examine one more episode: Ronnie had problems before he got to school. He and his mother had a disagreement and he arrives at school angry and upset. When Ms. Purvis greets Ronnie he just scowls and bulls his way into the room. He approaches the block area and pushes Byron to the floor. Byron complains verbally and kicks down a block tower. Ronnie then shoves Lesley into Grady. Grady pushes Lesley to the floor and punches Ronnie. At this moment, Eula is passing by with a doll in the baby buggy. Lesley tips over the buggy.

In the meantime Ronnie and Grady are having a first class fight. Grady hits Ronnie in the mouth and Ronnie screams, "You blooded me!" He feels his lip and confirms that there is a trace of blood. Crying loudly, Ronnie retreats toward Ms. Purvis for comfort. Meanwhile, the classroom is in shambles.

Unfortunately Ms. Purvis failed to notice that Ronnie was angry and upset. Had she recognized these signs early, she could have directed Ronnie to an activity away from other children until he felt better. Instead, Ronnie's anger contaiged the entire group.

Transitions and Movement Management

Teacher attributes include liking children, being creative and possessing knowledge in several subject matter areas. In addition the teacher needs to be an efficient manager.

In the average day a teacher may make 100 - 200 individual child contacts and supervise a dozen activity changes. Kounin (1970) observed that elementary classroom teachers averaged 33.2 major changes in learning activities in a single day! Thus, the teacher must be able to help children make many new shifts each day. These transitions not only require new materials but also entail a psychological alteration in one's frame of reference. These shifts can involve physically moving desks and tables; getting out new books; putting away play materials, plus cognitive shifts to problem solving, inductive reasoning and a host of other mental exercises.

In addition, the teacher must remain alert to individual and group needs. The school day should be well-balanced to offer variety, reduce boredom and maintain interest.

Kounin (1970) investigated movement management in great detail and the reader is referred to his research for a thorough analysis of this area. Kounin's categories related to movement include: smooth transitions, jerkiness, flip-flops and stimulus-bound events. In this section we will review these categories plus some additional areas which the writers feel are germane to good classroom management.

1. Transitions.

As indicated earlier, a teacher makes many transitions during the course of a day. Often the manner in which these transitions occur (smooth, jerky or abrupt) can effect the tone of the class.

For example: The class is outside on the playground. Ms. Sauls says, "All right children, it is time to go inside! Doris you will be the leader and start the line indoors."

In this example Ms. Sauls' influence technique is quite clear. It also possesses a certain definiteness and her directions are quite specific. The children will probably go inside without too much trouble.

Let us now examine a second observation: The class is outside on the playground. Ms. Schuler surveys the playground and says, "All right children, in five minutes we will go inside." Seeing that Diane and Robert are deeply involved with the outdoor blocks she adds, "Diane, you and Robert will have to stop in a couple of minutes so you will have time to pick up your blocks."

Like Ms. Sauls, Ms. Schuler's influence technique was quite clear. It was definite and specific. However, Ms. Schuler's overall transition (from outdoors to indoors) appears to be smooth. She surveyed the group and provided a warning. On the other hand, Ms. Saul's approach to the transition appears abrupt and jerky. But, we might ask, does this minor difference in approach to a transition really make any difference? Kounin's research would suggest that it can make a difference in children's behavior. Ms. Sauls appears to be "butting in" on the children's activities. Research suggests that jerky, abrupt transitions are more disturbing to children and create a situation more likely to contribute to deviant behavior. Certainly experienced teachers would advise: Whenever possible, give the children a "warning" in preparation for a change or transition in activities.

2. Stimulus-boundedness.

Kounin contrasted stimulus-boundedness with goal directed behavior. In a goal directed situation the teacher maintains her focus on a specific goal; in a stimulus-bound event the teacher reacts to some unplanned or irrelevant stimulus and is lured away from the original event.

For example: The teacher is at the blackboard explaining a math problem. She looks down one aisle and sees a piece of paper on the floor. She says, "Who dropped that paper on the floor? This room is becoming a pig pen." She walks over to the paper, looks at one of the children and says, "Henry, did you throw this paper on the floor?" Henry shakes his head and the teacher leans over and picks up the paper. She dramatically shows the paper to the class and says, "Here is a mystery for you. How could this piece of paper walk from someone's desk and find its way to the floor?"

Another example of "stimulus-bound" follows: Ms. Duggan is listening to Eva read aloud. As Eva is reading, Ms. Duggan is walking back and forth in front of the room. She looks up from her reading and notices the animal cage and exclaims, "Eunice Anne, you forgot to feed Harvey." Eva stops reading as Ms. Duggan goes to her desk and gets some rabbit pellets. She offers the pellets to Harvey saying, "I bet you are really hungry!"

Certainly there are situations which demand stopping a teaching activity. Often, however, teachers become "stimulus-bound" and distracted to some new situation which is totally irrelevant. In both examples presented there was class disruption — work activity stopped and children were impeded from continuing their academic pursuits. In both cases, however, the class disrupter — the work stopper — was not a deviant child. Rather, it was a "stimulus-bound" teacher.

3. Flip-Flops.

Kounin uses the term, "flip-flop" to describe the following situation. The teacher terminates one activity, starts another and then abruptly returns to the original activity.

For example, the teacher says, "Put away your arithmetic workbooks and get out your science books and turn to page 106." After the children have their science books open the teacher says, "How many of you finished your arithmetic problem?"

Another example of a flip-flop follows: The Hawks have finished their reading. The teacher says, "Okay, you may take your chairs and return to your tables." The children rise and start to return to their tables as directed. The teacher then says, "No wait . . . come on back and let's finish the story we started on Tuesday."

A flip-flop is actually a transition but it is jerky and abrupt. Also, like the stimulus-bound event, it is disruptive and prevents the class from progressing smoothly. Kounin's research would suggest that smooth transitions enhance work involvement and lessen deviancy.

4. Herding.

Some teaching experiences are reminiscent of the old Texas cattle drives. It involves moving children — from one table to another; from the homeroom to the bathroom; to the auditorium; to the music room; as well as daily trips to the playground. The teacher can devise methods which will ease movement problems and make transitions smooth. At times movement can be tied to concepts in problem solving. For example: "All who are wearing blue can go to the bathroom; all who are wearing green. . . . Monday's row may go; Tuesday's row. . . . "

On field trips peer arrangement may be a more crucial consideration. The teacher may wish to designate one child as leader (or head) of the line. The teacher will usually wish to hold the hands of specific children who may become frightened — or children who have a tendency to run and create a "child stampede!"

Significance Of Movement Management

Since so much of the school day is involved in movement management, it becomes a significant dimension in control and guidance in the classroom setting. Teachers who make abrupt transitions, flip flop and become stimulus-bound will experience discipline problems and general disruption. The teacher should carefully analyze her approach to change and transition. The importance of this area is emphasized by Kounin (1970, p. 108): "Techniques of movement management are more significant in controlling deviancy than are the techniques of deviancy management as such."

Pacing, Spacing and General Management Considerations

The teacher has been compared to an orchestra leader, the president of a business, an agent of culture, a maintenance man, a janitor, and a traffic cop. In many ways there are elements of all these tasks embodied in the teacher's role. The teacher has many functions to perform. In addition to guiding many activities throughout the day the teacher must "pace" the day to avoid satiation and boredom. She must be alert to the many activities which

126

are taking place simultaneously; she must be aware of both group and individual needs. All of these activities and materials must be considered in perspective or the teacher will find herself involved in "fighting windmills' and in "over-kill." This section will consider many of the general management considerations to which the teacher must remain ever alert.

1) Fighting Windmills.

There are a number of conditions which occur in life (and in the classroom) which could mercifully be termed "circumstance." Fighting windmills refers to situations in which the teacher may become upset over a condition which she is unable to control.

Examples of this situation are: Getting upset when the floor gets muddy on a rainy day. Trying to maintain absolute silence in the lunchroom because the principal enacted a law stating "No talking in the lunchroom." Taking children on a field trip and saying, "I want it so quiet I can hear a pin drop on this bus." Expecting children to be calm the day before the Christmas holidays.

There are many windmills in the teaching profession. If the teacher allows herself to become overly concerned, she can actually do damage to herself psychologically and physically. In the school setting, windmills usually occur in two areas: One — in the case of an administrative ruling over which the teacher has no control. The second exists in situations where one expects more of children than they can reasonably deliver. Our advice: Relax, "roll with the punches," try to maintain a sense of humor and some feeling of equilibrium.

Thus, children do get muddy shoes and they will get excited the day before Christmas. Talking at lunch is not deviant behavior; it is human behavior — and kids are like that — they are human.

2) Buildups and slow downs.

The teacher must be alerted to the overall pace of the

127

day. A day should be well-balanced so that vigorous activities are followed by a quiet period of time. Activities involving quick rapid strenuous physical movement should include periods where the child can relax and rest. A school day is not paced like the old TV show, "Laugh In." Children should not be expected to operate on a "high" the entire day. In many instances a deviancy problem may be related to pacing.

Let us observe the pacing (or level of activity) during a typical morning. Usually the activity level of a class starts slowly. As the morning progresses, however, the activity level (and the noise level) begins to build. One of the advantages of snack time is the opportunity it affords for a change of pace. It gives children a chance to slow down, relax and engage in quiet socialization. During the course of a busy morning the teacher may not have had occasion to speak to each.child. Snack time provides the teacher with a well-timed opportunity to interact with every individual.

Following snack period the activity level begins to build again. As lunch time approaches the activity level usually moves to a higher pitch. In addition, as children become hungry, frustration tolerance is lowered and tempers can flare. Just prior to lunch the teacher should plan some event (stories, songs, books, puzzles) which calm children down before going to eat.

Discipline and pacing are highly correlated. Problem situations arise when a group of children have been involved in vigorous activity over a period of time and find it difficult to slow down and "return to normal." Teachers should also carefully schedule activities so that children will not have extremely long waiting periods. Long waiting periods can be very frustrating to children and create unnecessary disturbances. Equally difficult are situations where children have remained quiet over a long period of time and have been unable to move about the classroom.

A teacher should have some "pace changing" activities in her repertoire. The purpose of the "pace changer" is to quickly alter the activity level of the class . . . thereby preventing a discipline or management problem. The teacher should learn several of these activities so well that she can institute them in a moment's notice. There are two general types of "pace changers" — one is designed to increase the activity level of the class; the other is designed to help the class lessen its pace.

Pace Changer Number One: Letting off steam. The purpose of this activity is to encourage children to move around, jump up and down and generally lessen the tensions which can build in a classroom setting. Ways of reducing tension include a simple running game or a song game which utilizes gross body movement.

There are times when a class has been engaged in an assignment involving concentration over a long period of time. In order to avoid satiation, the teacher may wish to change the pace for a few minutes and then return to the original activity. In this situation the teacher will wish to encourage movement, and yet maintain total control of the pace change. An example of this type of controlled activity is, "Simon Says." Notice the change of pacing in the following:

Simon says, "Wiggle your fingers."
Simon says, "Stretch your arms."
Simon says, "Run in place." (Then if the children become too boisterous . . .)
Simon says, "Stop running."
Simon says, "Tiptoe quietly to your seats."

In this type of activity the teacher can allow movement and activity. Yet the class remains in control when it is time to return to the original task.

Pace Changer Number Two: Putting the lid on. Tension can also build when young children are involved in highly active games or competitive events. Over an extended period they may become highly excited and over-stimulated. When this situation occurs the entire class can

129

quickly lose control and the group will seem to "fall apart." Even for the experienced teacher, returning to normalcy can be a difficult task.

Prior to the point where the class loses control, the teacher should begin initiating activities which lower the tension level. In some instances the teacher may wish to use a game (like "Simon Says") which will begin to restore control and order to the group. Then as the group "slows down" the teacher might read a story, lead the class in songs or encourage activities of a more sedentary nature.

A final important consideration in terms of pacing and timing is the preparation and celebration of major holidays. If a teacher begins to celebrate Christmas the first part of November, it will seem like an eternity before it arrives. This is particularly true for young children. It also keeps the class operating at a "fever pitch" for an extremely long period of time. Since children do not possess the temporal relations of adults, this situation also creates problems in the home.

3) Geographical considerations.

An important factor in behavior management concerns the placement of activities and materials within the classroom. General considerations for room arrangement include:

★ Traffic patterns
★ Noisy and quiet areas
★ Space for large and small group activity
★ Materials conveniently located
★ Movable furniture
★ Wet and dry areas
★ Locker placement
★ Window and door placement
★ Storage facilities
★ Color
★ Balance and order
★ Aesthetic appeal

In the fall of the year — before the opening of school, plan your overall traffic patterns and the areas which will be designated for different activities. The general considerations listed above will help you as you do your specific planning. In terms of placement of specific items and activities the following hints may be helpful. The block corner should not be adjacent to the music corner. Even the normal "noise" which accompanies block building is too disturbing for someone who is endeavoring to listen to phonograph records. (Note: A small carpet for blocks and transporation toys will reduce the noise significantly.)

Easels should be placed in a well-lighted area; near a window, if possible. Easels and fingerpaint tables should be located near a water source and there should be a drying rack nearby for hanging completed pictures. (Recently the writer visited a nursery school. The teacher of the four year olds had the easel paint drying rack across the room from the painting area. Hanging the pictures entailed walking the entire length of the room and through the doll corner. Not only was the rack inconvenient, the teacher disturbed the children in the doll corner each time she went to hang a picture.)

Be aware of the location of the sun throughout the school day. Will there be excessive glare on the desks; will the sun be in the children's eyes and interfere with their seeing the blackboard or participating in other activites?

How much material will be in the room when it is fully equipped? At times teachers forget how much space tables, chairs, easels, doll beds, blocks, etc. can consume. Then, when the room is completely furnished . . . there is no room for the children . . . or the room looks crowded, messy and unattractive.

The teacher should consider the placement of mats for rest period. Positioning of children is an equally important consideration. Children can become both physically and psychologically confined. When this situation arises, nerves become frayed — shoving, tussling and fighting soon follow.

4) Over-kill.

This technique refers to the teacher who makes a big issue out of some minor incident. The teacher engages in lecturing, preaching or moralizing to the class. Generally this technique disrupts the class, slows down the class activity and may actually cause deviant behavior to occur. The writers recall a classic example from summer camp.

The "Eagles" (a ten year old group of boys) are playing the "Women-Haters" (an eleven year old boy's group) in a spirited game of softball. Royce, the counselor for the Eagles is coaching from the sideline. Wally, one of his campers, is playing third base.

Royce: "Okay, Wally, let's look alive."

Wally: *(looks at Royce and smiles faintly.)*

Royce: "Come on, Wally, talk it up." *(twenty seconds pass)*

Royce: "Hey, Wally, get ready — move around."

Wally: *(shrugs shoulders)*

Royce: "Hey, Wally, get ready — this is a tough hitter —let's go!! Let's go!!"

The ball is hit to third base. Wally fields the ball and throws the batter out.

Royce: "All right, Wally, next time throw faster. He almost got on base."

Wally: *(frowning)* "Gosh, I got him out — what do you want?"

Royce: "Well, you could have missed him — look alive out there!" *(twenty seconds pass)*

Royce: "All right, Wally — get ready, talk to the pitcher, baby."

Wally: *(curls lip — says under his breath)* "Get off my back."

Royce: "What's that? Get on the ball, Wally . . . Tough batter . . . big stick?"

At this moment the batter rips a ground ball between Wally's legs. The runner advances safely to first base.

Royce: "Dammit, Wally . . . I told you to look alive. Get that apron down . . . you let them get a hit . . . get ready, baby, get ready!"

At this pont Wally removes his fielder's glove, throws it in the air, and rolls on the ground. Royce looks at the observer, throws up his hands and says, "What the hell did he do that for?"

In the classroom setting we can see "over-kill" in the following example:

Feron is slow in coming to the reading group. Ms. Waldrop says, "Feron you are a slow poke. You are always the last one to the reading group. Everyone has to wait while you dawdle and take your own sweet time." Ms. Waldrop looks over the room and says to no one in particular, "What would happen if everyone arrived late?" Ceclia says, "We wouldn't get our work finished." Ms. Waldrop, "That's right; Ceclia, we would never be finished. . . . What would have happened if Paul Revere was late?" *(no response)* "What would happen if your house were on fire and the firemen arrived late?" *(no response)*.

In this observation, the recorder commented that as the lecture on "being late" continued, the children were looking at the ceiling or the floor — and seemed to be purposefully avoiding the teacher's gaze. The observer also noted a slight undercurrent of noise. Often the preachments of "over-kill" disrupt the class and do not improve the behavior of the deviant child.

5) Self-help activities.

If you will closely examine your room and carefully plan your activities, there are many situations where children can perform tasks without teacher assistance.

Train yourself to view each task as a production engineer. You will be amazed at the number of tasks which children can do by themselves.

For example: Ms. Zeleny was the teacher of twenty-five, four year olds. She had one assistant, Ms. Kay. Dressing to go outside was a major hassle. Ms. Kay would take the "early dressers" (about three children) out of doors, leaving Ms. Zeleny with the rest of the group. The dressing room was very small. Fights broke out daily. There was always a mad scramble to get Ms. Zeleny to help. Finally Ms. Zeleny decided to approach her problem from a "production" point of view.

Each day Ms. Zeleny assigned several children to be "layout" assistants. Then, while she told the group a story, the layout personnel helped Ms. Kay place the clothing on the floor in the playroom. Each child's clothes were placed in a specific order. Snow pants first, then the boots, then the hat, followed by the coat and the mittens. The children enjoyed this activity and being chosen a layout assistant was considered an honor. Ms. Zeleny also alerted Ms. Kay to the importance of child placement. Children who were quite active were geographically separated to avoid fights. In addition, children who could dress themselves were placed next to children who could not . . . so the "dressers" could assist the "learners."

When the children started dressing to go outside, Ms. Zeleny and Ms. Kay were able to place themselves strategically. When a child was dressed, the teachers would show him another child he could help.

Dressing became an effective group management project instead of a teacher hassle. By making dressing an enjoyable experience in which children helped each other, there was a noticeable improvement in the *esprit de corps* of the total group.

Closely examine your room and your materials to determine ways where children can help themselves. Here are a few examples to guide your thinking:

★ *Clean up* — This suggestion is so basic that the teacher may feel it is unnecessary. Yet as we visit classrooms, we are appalled at the lack of "follow through" on the part of some teachers. Many teachers are continuously involved in picking up after children because they do not take the time to teach children their own responsibility for clean up after completing an activity. Granted, it does take time and patience to get children to learn this task. At times the teacher may need to offer encouragement and assist a child in this task. Children should learn (and the teacher should insist) that before moving to a new activity, they must pick up the material used in the previous activity. The teacher will save herself many precious minutes if she teaches children this basic rule in classroom management.

★ *Low shelves* — So children can reach the materials.

★ *Label shelves* — Label positions for materials so children can replace items after they have been used. Utilize pictures for nursery school and kindergarten children. This technique teaches children classification skills as well as learning to place things back in order.

★ *Bulletin boards* — Several children can be assigned the responsibility for decorating the bulletin board. Make sure the bulletin board is positioned so children can easily reach the board.

★ *Snack period* — Even two year old children can be taught to set up for snack period with some assistance. These children learn sets and one-to-one correspondence as they learn that each child receives one glass, one napkin, one placemat, one cookie. They learn sequencing when they see that the placemat must precede the glass, etc.

★ *Mixing paint and dough* — Teach children how to mix their own paint and assemble their own art materials. Containers should be used which are accessible and have snap lids.

★ *Library committee* — A library committee can be designated to choose books for the room.

★ *The new child* — It is often helpful to the teacher and security for a new child if he is assigned a "special friend" to help him "learn the ropes" at a new school.

★ *Parents help* — Parents can provide assistance in many ways. Parents can serve as "extra hands" on field trips, they can also assist in class on special days or school events. In addition, parents should be informed that there are many "little" ways in which the teacher can be helped. For example: Labelling clothing, purchasing galoshes amply large (Parents do not realize how frustrating it is when teacher and child have to struggle with a pair of tight overshoes.) The same is true for other items of wearing apparel . . . Coats sufficiently large for growing children; zippers that work; elastic pants; avoiding "Sunday" dress clothes; dressing the child in clothing that is washable.

★ *Operating equipment* — Young children can learn to operate a phonograph or a language master. Kindergarten children can operate headsets and a be trained to operate most AV and office equipment.

★ *Assign tasks* — Our own experience is that teachers usually do not realize how well children like responsibility and how well they can accept complex assignments. There are many tasks which children can perform which will significantly reduce teacher load. In the children's camp at The Merrill-Palmer Institute several years ago, campers were primarily responsible for every phase of camp life including planning activities, scheduling activities, menu planning, operation of the camp store, purchase of equipment and other camp functions. Younger children can dust, clean tables, distribute rest mats and other materials. They can even call the roll and check attendance. As children grow older they can collect money, take up tickets, assume responsibility for the care and feeding of plants and animals, tutor younger children in subject matter areas and help supervise the day of these youngsters.

★   *Cooperative planning* — A technique used successfully by many teachers is one of cooperative
planning of activities and routines. This approach
teaches children responsibility as well as providing
an introduction to democratic planning and discussion. We suggest that you choose a routine or
activity and lead a discussion with the children on
the goals of the activity, the requirements involved
and the responsiblity of the children involved. For
example you might select activities like using the
media center, going to the cafeteria, behavior in the
cafeteria, a fire drill or the child's own use of free
time. As the discussion progresses and all facets of
the topic are explored, the teacher can begin to
highlight the salient points by writing them on a
chalkboard or on a large sheet of chart paper. As
the discussion progresses, we suggest that you help
the students devise a list of specific goals and
responsibilities. After the discussion, the major
goal and the rules and responsibilities can be
summarized and placed on a large sheet of paper or
poster board.

For example, if you are writing a plan for a fire
drill, you might have as major goals, "To proceed
safely from the building and assemble at a safe
distance from the building. To insure that every
member of the class is out of the building." After
the goals have been established, you help the
children determine both individual and group
responsibilities necessary to achieve the goals and
the procedures involved in arriving at the goals.
(These might include: being careful as you leave the
room to avoid shoving or pushing; to walk on the
right side of the hallway to the appropriate exit; to
proceed to a certain area on the playground; to
form a circle, to call the roll, etc.) Insofar as
possible, state the rules in a positive manner.

After the planning sheet has been completed, it
can be hung in the room in a prominent place. Prior
to a fire drill, the teacher and pupils can review

the chart. Upon completion of the drill, the chart can again be studied to determine the extent to which the rules were followed and the goal or goals attained.

This approach to cooperative planning helps the teacher to pinpoint a particular problem and to show the group (or a specific individual) where the procedure broke down or went awry. Thus it serves as a vehicle for correction of a problem situation plus affording children the opportunity to participate in democratic planning and discussion. Abiding by rules made under democratic procedures lays the foundation for future self-discipline and responsibility.

6) Are you "with it"?

Kounin used the term "withitness," to describe a teacher who could demonstrate to her pupils — "I do know what is going on!" The competent teacher can communicate (often via non-verbal means) — "I am aware of what is happening; I am in control of the situation."

Every teacher knows that disruptive behavior will usually stop when the teacher moves in close geographical proximity to the deviant child. However, beginning teachers tend to forget this premise and do not place themselves strategically — or they become involved in one situation — and forget about the rest of the class.

In successful management of the clas the teacher who is "with it" is capable of juggling the multi-faceted situational variables which prevail at any given moment in the school day.

In this book we have examined many factors which are necessary for good discipline and management control. Current research and clinical observation would suggest that there is a "Discipline and Classroom Management" syndrome composed of behaviors which are used by teachers who are successful. To cite all these behaviors would involve reviewing the entire book. However, some factors seem so significant we would like to summarize the salient features of this syndrome:

Discipline and Classroom Management Syndrome.
* ★ There is no substitute for good teaching. When subject matter is stimulating and enjoyable, the teacher will experience few discipline problems.
* ★ Children do learn by modeling. Children model their behavior after the adult who teaches them.
* ★ How you were reared as a child; the influence techniques used by your parents, your teachers; how you feel about discipline — all relate directly to your own attitudes and beliefs about discipline. Your attitudes have a direct relationship to the discipline techniques which will be successful for you.
* ★ Recognize that human behavior is very complex. Often the causes for behavior may not be immediately apparent, but have their roots in physical, cultural or social factors which indirectly influence classroom behavior.
* ★ The emotional climate in which discipline occurs is more significant than the technique used.
* ★ Management techniques — particularly those involved with transitions and classroom change — are more significant in controlling deviancy than discipline techniques as such.
* ★ In managing the classroom, the teacher recognizes the value of organization and preplanning. The day should be planned well ahead of the children's arrival so the teacher has the time to greet the children and get them started toward a productive day. In preplanning the teacher considers:
  — balance of activities
  — variety of activities
  — pacing
  — individual and group needs
  — short and long range goals

★ In utilizing influence techniques, the teacher recognizes the importance of:
  — clarity
  — consistency
  — firmness
  — positive statements

★ An influence technique will be improved if the teacher uses her "power" with a cushion — e.g., offering an alternative; an explanation; a reason.

★ Children learn in accordance with the rules of reinforcement theory. Praising a child for appropriate behaviors, increases the likelihood that the desired behaviors will continue.

★ Reward appropriate behavior *after* it occurs. Grandma's rule states, "First you do what I want you to do, then you may do what you wish to do." Usually the child will work for the opportunity to engage in an activity he enjoys.

★ Reward the total class for appropriate behavior. Often the teacher takes good behavior for granted, but punishes incorrect behavior.

External And Internal Discipline

Very early in life the infant learns that discipline is external to his own being. Even when he is very demanding, the control he exerts over his parents is entirely volitional — they can do as they wish; they establish the rules and they enforce them. It should be recognized, however, that in the case of the very young child the parent often has no other workable alternative. If a two year old is playing with a bottle of furniture polish, the parent will prohibit this activity. She will not consult the child and reach a democratic decision. This is as it should be . . . no two year old is capable of understanding the dangers involved . . . nor should he be consulted in the decision making process.

External discipline — while it may be very necessary —is not without problems, however. It is usually effective only to the extent that the authority figure (who imposed the rule) is capable of inflicting punishment.

For example, if the two year old is slapped every time he touches furniture polish, he will not touch the bottle under two conditions:

a) He sees the authority is present and knows that he will be slapped for his behavior.

b) He sees the authority is not present but the child fears she will appear. If the authority figure appears, condition (a) will prevail.

Given the previous example, the child's ability to discipline himself is based on circumstances which are external to him. In this instance, he will avoid the furniture polish because of fear of the authority figure.

In the final analysis, however, discipline must be considered in a larger context than merely in terms of reward and punishment. In order to be effective during those periods when the authority figure is absent, discipline must have meaning for the child.

When the child is older, the adult can explain the dangers inherent in a bottle of furniture polish. Once the child understands this fact he will refrain from playing with the polish because the reasons are meaningful to him. Under these circumstances — when discipline has become internalized — the authority figure does not need to be present.

Self-discipline begins to occur when the adult provides reasons for rules and regulations. Unfortunately, as cited in this book, adults often give prohibitions — but they seldom offer reasons.

In less potentially dangerous situations, children should be afforded the opportunity to learn rules through discovery as they explore and experiment on their own. Rules about living with others and working with others are often best learned in this fashion.

For example, Ms. Paguio was having difficulty with the

concept of sharing in her first grade class. Usually the children resolved the problem of sharing via brute force. After a few weeks the teacher realized she had become the final arbitrator in most of the classroom disputes.

One day, during group time, Ms. Paguio raised this problem with the children. During the ensuing discussion the children compiled a list of "rules for sharing." One child suggested that these "rules" be posted on the bulletin board to serve as a reminder to everyone. After the children had agreed on the rules for sharing, disputes noticeably declined.

Children usually display pride and a feeling of esprit de *corps* when they share in making rules. The teacher should enlist the aid of the class in making rules which effect everyone.

Every time we help children learn to cope with a problem and to handle their feelings, we move them one step closer to mastering self-discipline. Self-discipline implies self-respect for others.

Children can begin to learn social responsibility early. Although they are highly egocentric — and while it is difficult to see another's point of view — very young children can begin to share and interact with others. If children are to learn social responsibility there must be many opportunities to test and to try; to succeed and to fail.

A major task for the parent and teacher is to structure the environment so that the child can begin to direct his own behavior within that environment and learn to live with the consequences of his own actions. Ideally, self-discipline is learned at home and in the classroom. In these situations the adult can create a climate which is basically trusting and friendly.

In the final analysis, the teacher is trying to "work herself out of the business of discipline." In a democratic society authority figures do not follow people around enforcing rules, dispensing tokens and inflicting punishments. Thus, as the child grows into adulthood, he must develop an internal discipline. He ultimately learns to behave in an appropriate fashion — but not because of the

142

teachers, policemen, parents and other reinforcers in society. . . . He behaves appropriately because he lives in a society which respects fairness and honesty for oneself and for others.

Learning Objectives For Chapter Seven:

After reading Chapter Seven, "Techniques of classroom management," the reader should be able to:

1. Identify the single most important factor in controlling classroom behavior.
2. Identify contagion in a classroom and predict its effects.
3. Understand and grasp the significance of movement management and transitions in controlling classroom behavior.
4. Given a situation reflecting a problem in management or transition, the reader should be able to recognize an example of a stimulus-bound event, a "flip-flop," a problem of pacing and offer suggestions to improve the classroom management situation.
5. Given a discipline problem related to the classroom environment, the reader should be able to analyze potential difficulties in room arrangement and make concrete suggestions for change.
6. Give examples of student "self-help" activities which can alleviate some potential discipline problems.

7. Differentiate between internal and external discipline and discuss the value of each type. Explain the problems which can arise with external discipline.
8. Without the aid of references, list and discuss _____ major factors which are necessary for good discipline and classroom management. (The text described *twelve* major factors; the reader can set her own criterion for adequate knowledge of this item.)
9. Define the following terms:
   a. contagion effect
   b. transitions
   c. stimulus-bound events
   d. flip-flops
   e. herding
   f. fighting windmills
   g. over-kill
   h. pace changers
   i. withitness
   j. internal discipline
   k. external discipline

Appendices

Appendix A

Positive Verbal and Nonverbal Reinforcers

. . . "One liners" that turn kids on . . .

Every child needs praise and positive reinforcement. He needs to know the teacher cares for him as a person and recognizes his feelings and accomplishments. Unfortunately, adults often fail to reinforce desired behavior. At times we fall into the rut of using general vocabulary which does not meaningfully describe appropriate behavior or accomplishments. Teachers often say, "You are a good boy," when it would be more appropriate to describe the exact behavior or state specifically why the teacher is satisfied. For example, "You have really improved — you got all the problems correct!"

At times it is not what one says but how they say it. Positive reinforcements should be sincere, honest and enthusiastic. Some teachers utilize positive verbal reinforcers effectively, but may forget how effective the nonverbal gestures can be. Smiling, laughing, nodding, a pat on the back, or being close to a child can serve as powerful reinforcements. The teacher who learns to utilize verbal and nonverbal reinforcers will find them helpful in discipline and classroom management.

The following "one liners" and gestures are given as a beginning repertoire:

Teacher satisfaction – Verbal reinforcers

Thank you very much.
You are very thoughtful.
I appreciate your help.
That's wonderful!
Good for you, _____.
Great — Hey, that's great!
That's attractive.
You are tops.
That's a great idea.
I'm happy for you.
You are a gem, pearl, plum, etc.
You win first place for that.
I'm glad you did.
That's pretty.
That's top notch.
You're one in a million.
That's really helpful.
I'm so pleased.
I'm ticked pink.
I'm so glad.
I'm pleased as punch.

Terrific
Super
Wow
Super duper
Wise choice
Splendid
Keen
Fine and dandy
Jam-up
Thrilled
Hmmm!
Hot digity!
Splendid
Fantastic
Excellent
Neat
Magnificent
Grand
Swell
Nifty
O-Kay!
Goody
Hot dog
Oh boy!

Verbal reinforcers which acknowledge child's accomplishments or ability

I can tell you are trying.
That's creative.
I can tell you are thinking.
I wish everybody could do _____!
You're a good problem solver — you can _____.
You worked hard on _____.
Your effort is evident.
I like the way you think.
I like the way you try.
I like the way you work.
I wish every room could see that — let's put it in the hall.
Let's show _____ to the principal or teacher down the hall or next level teacher, etc.
You did so well, you're ready to _____.

146

That's your best work!
You followed directions.
You do that so well.
You are really fast.
I can see you took your time to do that correctly.
You are doing much better.
You got it.
I like your drawing, it _____.
Hey, you got _____ correct!
Keep up the good work.
That's better.
You're a good worker — you _____.
You are really improving.
You are smart to think of _____.
You have your thinking cap on.
You are to be commended.

Verbal reinforcers for the entire class.

When the class is quiet, we can all work more effectively!
I see _____ is waiting quietly.
I'm glad to see so many helpers.
You are such good listeners.
I like the way you share.
I see _____ is ready to get started with _____.
Let's see how many are ready to go to lunch (then name specific ones).

Verbal reinforcers which acknowledge child's feelings

I know you are happy inside.
You seem very happy doing that.
You seem pleased with yourself.
I can see you are really turned on.
You are happy as a lark, king, etc.
I can tell you are satisfied.
I know you are glad that _____.
That makes you tingle.
You are really flying high.
I know you enjoyed that.

Nonverbal reinforcers

Being near a child
Touching a child
Patting
Hugging
Holding a child's hand

Smiling
Winking
Looking up
Raising eyebrows
Nodding head

Laughing
Clapping
Snapping fingers
Swinging arms
Hand gestures
Thumbs up — "Fonz"
OK signal

Appendix B

Interest Finder Chart

The teacher can construct a chart listing activities which can serve as reinforcers for children in her classroom. She can mark activities which each child enjoys or have children indicate their preference for a given activity. Ratings are shown in terms of high, moderate or low interest.

	Activity	Circle Level		
1.	Easel Painting	H	M	L
2.	Lotto games	H	M	L
3.	Language Master	H	M	L
4.	Puzzles	H	M	L
5.	Crayons	H	M	L
6.	Collage	H	M	L
7.	Woodworking	H	M	L
8.	Filmstrip	H	M	L
9.	Weaving	H	M	L
10.	Sitting with a friend	H	M	L
11.	Lincoln Logs	H	M	L
12.	Water & Sand Table	H	M	L
13.	Blockbuilding	H	M	L
14.	Record Player	H	M	L
15.	Free Choice	H	M	L

Appendix C

Observational Analysis

The text has discussed the importance of observations to help the teacher ascertain problems and probable solutions. Several anecdotal observations are included in this section. We would suggest that the student study these "samples" and construct some hypotheses concerning the participants in the observations. Students may also wish to discuss how they would change the behaviors noted in these observational vignettes.

Observation #1. Camp Setting[1]

The following observation was taken verbatim from a group of eight ten year old boys in a camp setting. Note that each statement is numbered — following the observation an analysis is made of the interaction. The Counselor (Cs) is discussing kinds of possible program activities with the group:

1. Cs: O.K., I'm ready — come over here and sit down. I'm open to suggestions.
2. Adam: Let's pack supper and go on an overnight hike.
3. Cs: H'm-m-m. . .

---

[1]This observation was originally presented in a speech published by the Southern Association for Children Under Six. The speech was entitled, "Three Characters in Search of a Plot".

150

4. Bill: Let's have a Nature Hike.
5. Cs: That's a good idea. What do we need for a nature hike?
6. Dick: We need six-twelve for mosquitoes.
7. Adam: How about an overnight hike?
8. Cs: One at a time — what else do we need for a nature hike?
9. Peter: We could ask Joy (the nature counselor) to go with us and point out the flowers and leaves.
10. Cs: That's a good idea ...That would be quite educational. What else for the nature hike?
11. Mitch: How about "Capture the Flag"?
12. Cs: H'm-m-m ...Tom, aren't you going to contribute? These ideas must come from everyone.
13. Tom: "Capture the Flag."
14. Cs: Somebody has already mentioned that Now what else do we need to know for our nature hike?
15. Dick: Take canteens, knives and hatchets.
16. Cs: Fine. Now, shall we go swimming and boating?
17. All: Yeah.
17a Cs: Swimming?
    All: Yes, let's go swimming (consensus).
18. Cs: Boating?
19. Adam: How about an overnight hike?
20. Cs: We are voting for boating now. Who wants boating?
21. All: Yeah, Okay (consensus).
22. Cs: Good, that's settled. Any suggestions for outside games?
23. Bill: Let's play ball with Pedro's Cabin.
23a.   Adam leaves the group at this point and starts for the door of the cabin.
24. Cs: Where are you going, Adam? We need everyone's help on program planning.
25. Adam: I'm going to the bathroom (leaves).
26. Cs: Okay ...well, I guess we are all set now. Someone better go over to Pedro's Cabin and

151

see if they want to play ball with us tomorrow.

(Note: The recorder stopped at this point.)

Analysis and Comment

A superficial glance would indicate that the discussion taking place was held in a democratic fashion. A quick tabulation would indicate that six of the eight children in the group made contributions to the discussion. A cursory examination also reveals (items 17 and 21) that the group voted. Items 2, 7, and 19 indicate "opportunity" for a minority opinion to be voiced. Thus we see the elements of the democratic process in action: discussion, voting, minority and majority opinion. Unfortunately, closer examination reveals that our example of democracy never advanced beyond the elements.

One item which becomes immediately apparent in the group discussion is the overwhelming domination of the group leader. This can be seen in several ways: (a) The group leader made 13 or the 26 responses during the discussion. (Note: In five days of observing this group, the leader made approximately 45 percent of the responses during the group discussion.) (b) Both conscious (items 8, 14, and 20) and unconscious (item 3) statements are made to the group in an effort to rebuff certain suggestions from group members. (c) From item 1 to item 16 we observe a move on the part of the leader from hearing suggestions and exploring possibilities to a final decision. Item 16 indicates the leader has made a decision without any group consensus. Items 5, 8, and 10 seem only tools which the leader manipulates in order to move the group to his own ends. (d) Of the four activities suggested (nature hike, swimming, boating, outside games) only one came from the group per se.

A second unfortunate consequence is Adam. Constantly rebuffed by the leader, he finally leaves the situation. (Item 23A.) Items 12 and 24 also reveal a very disturbing factor these statements indicate a verbal acceptance of the democratic process on the part of the leader. One can conjecture that while the leader is actually forcing group decisions, he

152

seems to be of the opinion that he is getting group decision and participation.

One final note: The results of this type of group management seem best summed up with the following incident which occurred about a week later. At breakfast two of the boys approached one of the authors and the following conversation took place:

Peter: We are going on a hot dog roast tonight.
K.O.:   Hey, that's nice! Where will you go?
Peter: I don't know.
Adam: The counselor knows . . .That's all that matters.

Observation #2. Observation of juice period.

The Head Teacher of a four year old group approached us with a problem. As she remarked: "Our snack period is very hectic. No one seems to stop or even slow down."

We observed the snack period for ten consecutive days. One of these observations is presented below. The pacing and verbal content is typical of all ten observations.

The teacher has set up the juice table in the corner of the room. Grape juice and crackers have been placed on the table. The teacher has poured the juice from a large pitcher into two smaller ones. Some of the children have already had their juice as the observation begins.

1. T: "Everybody come and get juice."
2. Susan: "This just makes me hungrier." Drinks juice.
3. T: "Why don't you have some more?"
4. Susan: Pours another glass and says, "This just makes me hungrier."
5. T: Jimmie runs near the table. T. says, "Jimmie, go wash your hands and have some juice."
6.   Colus runs by the table, picks up a cracker and runs off.
7. T: "Everybody come and get juice."
8. T: "Sean, come have juice now."
9. Sean: "I have had it already."
10. T: "Maria, do you want a cup?"

11.		Maria does not reply verbally but accepts the juice from the teacher.
12.	T:	"Everybody come and get juice."
13.	Carol:	*(Shouting)* "Everybody come and get juice." Then in a more subdued tone, "I'm gonna take two cups." She fills two cups and spills some juice on the table. She quickly gulps down both cups and leaves the table.
14.		Teacher cleans up the juice which Carol spilled.
15.	T:	Tanya comes near the table. T. hands Tanya a pitcher and says, "Have some juice."
16.	Amos:	"I want some juice."
17.	T:	"Here is a pitcher."
18.	Amos:	"It's empty."
19.	T:	Goes over to the sink and gets another small pitcher of juice. Returns to the table and gives the pitcher to Amos saying, "Here you are, more juice."
20.	T:	"Last call, did everyone get their juice?"

Analysis and Comment:

In this observation one can sense the feeling of disorganization during the snack period. Notice that the overall "theme" in the teacher's verbal behavior seems to be: "Everyone come and get juice." In this report there are twelve separate items of teacher interaction. Unfortunately every item refers specifically to juice and crackers. The teacher makes no effort to positively reinforce "sitting behavior" or social interchange.

Item 14 suggests that the teacher might have asked Carol to clean up. Instead, the teacher performs this task herself. Item 13 deserves special mention: In this item we see Carol model the teacher's verbal behavior.

Observation #3. Classroom Setting.

The following observation was taken in a classroom of first grade children. The children have just come in from recess. The teacher is planning to start an arithmetic lesson.

154

As the observation begins the class is very noisy and the children are wandering about the classroom.

1. T: "Everybody get in their seats and get quiet!"
2. T: *(thirty seconds passes)* Teacher goes over to the light switch and switches the overhead light out for several seconds. *(very loud, almost shouting)* "Do you know what lights out mean?" There is no noticeable change in classroom noise level.
3. T: Switches lights on and off rapidly four times. Do you know what lights out mean?"
4. Amy: "Ms. Morton, may I go get a drink of water?"
5. T: Amy, I am trying to get this class quiet . . .no, you may not go get water yet."
6.   Amy walks back near the door . . .when the teacher is not looking, Amy scoots out the door.
7. T: "I am still waiting for quiet."
8.   During this period Scott and Dante are in a scuffle over a paper clip. Scott gets it and twists it into the shape of a gun.
9. T: *(switches lights)* "Do you know what lights out mean?"
10.   Two children are under a table. The teacher approaches them and says, "Robert you and Camille go stand in the hall and get quiet!" *(Pause . . .then in a loud voice)* . . ."Everybody get in your seats!"
11. Scott: "Dante isn't in his seat!"
12. T: "Okay, Scott, you told me . . .Get in your seat, Dante . . .Everybody, please close your mouth.
13. T: *(thirty seconds passes)* "Everybody freeze!" '
14.   Most children stop for a few seconds at this command . . .but quickly the activity begins to pick up again.
15. T: "You are not paying attention . . .I know some boys that don't know the meaning of following directions."

155

16.	T:	Goes to the light switch. Flips lights. "I am going to count to three. I am sure I can think of some extra writing you can do."
17.	T:	"One ...two ...three ...extra writing for Gary, Shane and Scott." Scott and Shane go to their seats.
18.		Amy returns to the room.
19.	T:	"Amy, take your seat."
20.	T:	Most children are now in their seats. The teacher says, "Let's all count to ten."
21.		Children count to ten in unison.
22.	T:	"Gary, take your seat."
23.	Robert:	*(from in the hallway).* "Ms. Morton, will you give us another chance?"
24.	T:	"Robert, you are going to have to stay out there and be quiet."
25.	T:	"Let's all turn to page 93 in our math book." *(Observer's note: Although most children are in their seats, few are paying attention most of the children are still talking. Two boys crawl under a table. They are under the table for three minutes.)*
26.	T:	"Gil, get out from under the table!"
27.	T:	Shannon goes to the front of the room, gets some animal crackers and starts passing them out to the children.
28.	T:	"Shannon, I did not ask you to pass out animal cookies ...we are doing arithmetic now."

Analysis and Comment:

Obviously this teacher is experiencing some management difficulties in restoring order to the class and in making a transition to arithmetic. Analysis of this observation is being omitted to provide the reader with an opportunity to diagnose the management problems and offer some suggestions on how the teacher could improve. *(Hint: Start by counting the number of positive reinforcements in the observation.)*

Appendix D

Ratings, Contracts and Assessment

The following items are designed to help you assess yourself and your teaching by: a) analyzing the source of your problems in maintaining discipline, and b) determining if you are meeting your overall goals.

Keep a "problem log."

We suggest the following procedure: At the beginning of the school day, designate a specific problem or area which you wish to record for that day's session. In some cases you may wish to keep the log on a specific problem for several days. The following problems or areas may help you to evaluate your specific shortcomings in discipline or classroom management:

a) Make a list of specific problems you encountered today. How did you handle the problems? Were you clear? consistent? firm?

b) Keep track of prohibitions which you "meted out" to students. Do you have too many rules? Are your rules too picky? (Remember: The more rules you have, the more rules students will break.) Did you offer the students an alternative? Did you provide a "cushion"?

c) Make a list of specific students with whom you have difficulty in setting firm limits.

d) List your three "most difficult" students. Itemize their specific problems. Map out some strategies of ways you can help these students with their problems.

e) List two or three situations which were upsetting to you today. Try to determine the reason or reasons that these events upset you. (Hint: Re-read the section entitled, "Am I the Problem?")

f) What methods did you use to communicate to students that you were dissatisfied with their performance? Were you clear and specific — did they really understand the source of the problem?

g) Did you help children to understand and accept the consequences of their actions? Did you follow through?

h) What positive reinforcers did you use? Were they effective? Were you consistent in your reinforcements?

i) Did you make contact with all of the students today? Did all the students *know* (through your recognition and assurance) that you were aware of their presence today and interested in their activities? Did you avoid any problem children? Did you forget to notice the "quiet child"?

Examining a specific problem.

(Note: Re-read Chapter One. Some of the material below is taken from that chapter.)

a) Describe the child's problem or problems. (Study the section on "Determining the Problem" in Chapter One.) What specific behavior or behaviors are inappropriate? What changes need to be made in order to obtain behaviors which will be acceptable? What do you plan to do if you do not get acceptable behavior?

b) Ask yourself: Am I the problem? Is there something that I am doing which is contributing to this child's behavior.

c) Does the child have a physical problem? What is the

child's learning ability? Am I expecting too much? Is there some unknown situation in the home or the school environment? Is there a developmental problem? What is the child's role in the peer group?

Student Ratings of the Teacher

Some teachers may wish to design a rating scale so that children can rate the teacher's performance in certain areas. You can devise items in terms of your discipline, your general teaching skills, specific subject matter skills as well as personality attributes.

Prior to having students do the rating, the teacher should discuss the purpose of ratings — their advantages and their shortcomings. Of course, the ratings should be anonymous if they are to be truly effective. Two typical formats and sample items are presented below:

DIRECTIONS:

Below are some items for you to rate. Circle the response that most nearly presents your feelings. Remember that you do not have to place your name on the paper, so be completely honest in your evaluation.

Circle the Correct Response:

1) Generally my teacher is:
    Very friendly   Friendly   Not too friendly

2) Our math lesson was:
    Very interesting   So-so   Fair   Boring

3) Our homework assignments are:
    Too Long   About Right   Too Short

DIRECTIONS:

I would like to know how you feel about our Interest Centers. Would you please place an "x" in the box which most nearly represents your feelings? Remember you do not have to identify yourself, so please give me your honest opinion.

ITEM	Excellent	Very Good	Okay	Fair	Poor
Reading Center					
Math Center					
Science Center					
Art Center					

Contracts

Contracts are used in many phases of everyday life. A contract is a binding agreement between two individuals and states certain conditions which must be met. Utilizing Skinner's theory of operant conditioning, some researchers in the area of behavior modification have employed contracting.

There are situations when students find work uninteresting and have little motivation to carry out a specific assignment. Contracting is one technique which has proved helpful in getting the work accomplished. Contracting is a method for individualizing class instruction as well as helping students maintain interest. The steps to take are as follows: a) Keep the contract simple. We have seen some contracts which appear to be worded by a "Philadelphia Lawyer." b) The teacher and pupil agree on the specific area to be covered by the contract. (Studies in this area suggest: The contract should be jointly determined — with the student taking an integral part in determining the task and conditions of the contract — the contract should not be a unilateral document. The contract should be based on a small task and one which can be completed within a relatively short period of time.) c) The contract should clearly state the conditions: For example: "When ten math problems are completed correctly, the student may work with puppets, use the Language Master or look at filmstrips for the remainder of the period." d) The teacher should observe the student to make sure that the contract is being fulfilled. e) It is advisable to set a "completion date" when the contract will be terminated and a new contract can be negotiated.

There can be problems with contracting: Sometimes there is high interest on the part of the student, but after the initial enthusiasm wears off, the old problem remains and the teacher is back where she started.

Some teachers may feel that this type of arrangement is just a technique to manipulate the student or it represents a sophisticated bribe. (It should be pointed out that most of us *do* sign contracts for our work.) There are instances when the adult may need to provide "extrinsic rewards" until the child learns the joys of doing a particular task. When this has occurred, the child will accomplish the task for its own intrinsic reward.

Appendix E

Glossary Of Drug Terms

Acid	LSD
Acidhead	(also hop head) Frequent user of LSD
Angel dust	PCP
Bag, lid	Packet of drugs. (In grass: 3/4 ounce.)
Bennies	Benezedrine
Blue angels	Amytal
Bummer (Bum trip)	Bad experience with psychedelics
Burnout	Person who is "burned out" on drugs.
Candy	Barbiturates
Cannabis	Scientific name for grass
Clean	Off drugs
Coke	Cocaine
Cold turkey	Off drugs, withdrawal from drugs
Cut	Dilute drugs by adding milk sugar
Dexies	Dexedrine
Dope	Depressant drug
Downers	Sedatives
Drop	Swallow a drug

Fix	Injection of narcotics
Footballs	Amphetamines
Freakout	Bad drug experience
Gluey	Person who inhales glue
Good trip	Good experience with psychedelics
Goofballs	Sleeping pills
Grass	Marijuana (also called: Pot, weed, reefer, dope, rope, Mary Jane, MJ)
H	Heroin
Hard stuff	Heroin
Hash	Hashish, the resin of Cannabis
Head Shop	Store which sells drug related items
Hearts	Dexedrine tablets
Heat	Police
High	Under the influence. (Also called: Stoned, buzzed, fried, bombed out.)
Hooked	Addicted
Horse	Heroin
Hype	Drug addict
Joint	Marijuana cigarette
Jolly beans	Pep pills
Junkie	Addict
Kick the habit	Stop drug usage
Ludes	Quaaludes
M	Morphine
Mainline	Inject drug into veins
Manicure	Remove dirt, sticks, seeds from pot
Monkey	Morphine
Narco (Narc)	Narcotics agent
Nickel bag	$5.00 package of drugs. (Dime: $10.00 package.)
O.D.	Drug overdose
Poly-user	Uses several drugs (Poly Party: Gathering where several drugs are being used.)

163

Pep pills	Amphetamines
Pop	Inject drugs
Purple hearts	Dexamyl
Pusher	Drug dealer
Rainbows	Tuinal (red and blue capsule)
Red devils (Reds)	Seconal
Reefer	Marijuana cigarette
Roach	Marijuana butt
Scag	Heroin
Score	Make a drug purchase
Shoot	Inject durgs
Shooting gallery	Place where addicts gather
Skin popping	Injecting drugs under the skin
Smack	Heroin
Snort	Inhale drugs (usually cocaine)
Snow	Cocaine
Speed	Methedrine
Speedfreak	Addicted to methedrine
Stash	Supply of drugs hidden in safe place
Strung out	Addicted
Stuff	Any drug
Sugar	Cube of LSD
TCH	Main chemical in marijuana
Tea	Marijuana
Tripping out	Getting high on psychedelics
Turned on	Under the influence
Uppers	Stimulants
Yellow jacket	Nembutal

Suggested References

Bandura, A. *Aggression: A social learning theory analysis.* Englewood Cliffs: Prentice Hall, 1973.

Becker, W. *Parents are teachers.* Champaign, IL: Research Press, 1975.

Bee, H. *The developing child.* New York: Harper & Row, 1981.

Caldwell, B. M. Aggression and hostility in young children. *Young Children,* 1977, *32,* 4-13.

Cohen, D., & Stern, V. *Observing and recording the behavior of young children.* New York: Teachers College Press, 1958.

Diebert, A., & Harmon, A. *New tools for changing behavior.* Champaign, IL: Research Press, 1971.

Dittman, L. The mentally retarded child. In *Childcraft: Guide for parents.* Chicago: Field Enterprises Educational Corp., 1981. (vol. 15).

Dreikurs, R., Grunwald, B., & Pepper, F. *Maintaining sanity in the classroom: Illustrated teaching techniques.* New York: Harper & Row, 1971.

Dunaway, J. How to cut discipline problems in half. In *Discipline: Day by Day.* Washington: NEA, nd. (cassettes)

Elardo, R., & Caldwell, B. Value imposition in early childhood: Fact or fancy? *Child Care Quarterly,* 1973, *10,* 6-13.

Epstein, C. *Classroom management and teaching.* Reston, VA: Reston Publishing Co., 1980.

Fleming, R. The supervisor as an observer. In Beegle, C., & Brandt, R. (Eds.), *Observational methods in the classroom.* Washington: ASCD, 1973.

Gearheart, B., & Weishahn, M. *The handicapped child*

in the regular classroom. St. Louis: C. V. Mosby Co., 1976.

Gnagey, W. *Controlling classroom misbehavior.* Washington: NEA, 1969 (filmstrip also available).

Gordon, I. *Studying the child in school.* New York: John Wiley, 1966.

Gordon, T. *T.E.T. Teacher effectiveness training.* New York: Peter Wyden, 1974.

Hetherington, M., & Deur, J. The effects of father absence on child development. *Young Children,* 1971, *26,* 233-244.

Kephart, N. *The slow learner in the classroom.* Columbus: C. E. Merrill, 1974.

Kounin, J. *Discipline and group management in classrooms.* New York: Holt, Rinehart and Winston, 1970.

Kounin, J., & Gump, P. The ripple effect in discipline. *The Elementary School Journal,* 1958, *35,* 158-162.

Murphy, L., & Leeper, E. *Away from bedlam.* Washington: HEW Publication No. (OHD) 75-1029, 1974.

Ofchus, L. T. *Effects on non-target classmates of teachers' efforts to control deviant behavior.* Unpublished doctoral dissertation, Wayne State University, 1960.

Osborn, D. K. *Saliencies in students' perceptions of teachers.* Unpublished doctoral dissertation, Wayne State University, 1962.

Osborn, D. K. Permissiveness re-examined. In M. Rasmussen (Ed.), *Readings in Childhood Education.* Washington: ACEI, 1968.

Read, M. *Malnutrition, learning and behavior.* Washington: NICHD Publication No. (NIH) 76-1036, 1976.

Rheingold, H., Gewirtz, J., & Ross, H. Social conditioning of vocalizations in the infant. *J. Comparative Physiological Psychology,* 1959, *52,* 68-74.

Rowen, B. *The children we see.* New York: Holt, Rinehart and Winston, 1973.

Sears, R., Maccaoby, E., & Levin, H. *Patterns of Child*

Rearing. Evanston: Row, Peterson and Co., 1957.

Sigel, I., Hoffman, M., Dreyer, A., & Torgoff, I. Influence techniques used by parents to control the behavior of children. *American Journal of Orthopsychiatry,* 1957, *27,* 356-364.

Skeen, P., & McKenry, P. The teacher's role in facilitating a child's adjustment to divorce. *Young Children,* 1980, *35,* 3-12.

Sloane, H. *Classroom management: Remediation and prevention.* New York: John Wiley and Sons, 1976.

Smith, J., & Smith, D. *Child management: A program for parents and teachers.* Champaign: Research Press, 1976.

Volknor, C., Langstaff, A., & Higgins, M. *Structuring the classroom for success.* Columbus: C. E. Merrill, 1974. (filmstrips.)

Wallen, C., & Wallen, L. *Effective classroom management.* Boston: Allyn & Bacon, 1978.

Walker, J., & Shea, T. *Behavior modification: A practical approach for educators.* St. Louis: C. V. Mosby Co., 1980.